WOMEN IN THE ANCIENT NEAR EAST

THE IMAGE OF WOMAN

ILSE SEIBERT

WOMEN IN THE ANCIENT NEAR EAST

ABNER SCHRAM
NEW YORK

Translated from the German by Marianne Herzfeld, revised
by Professor George A. Shepperson
We also want to thank Miss M. Downie for her assistance

Published in the United States of America
by Abner Schram (A Division of Schram Enterprises)
1860 Broadway, New York, N.Y. 10023
ISBN 0-8390-0149-5
Copyright © 1974 by Edition Leipzig
Library of Congress Catalog Card Number: 74-10448
Printed in Germany (East)

CONTENTS

*The present book provides a survey of women's life in the Ancient
Near East, especially in the following areas: Asia Minor, the Syrian-
Palestinian region and present-day Iraq and Iran*

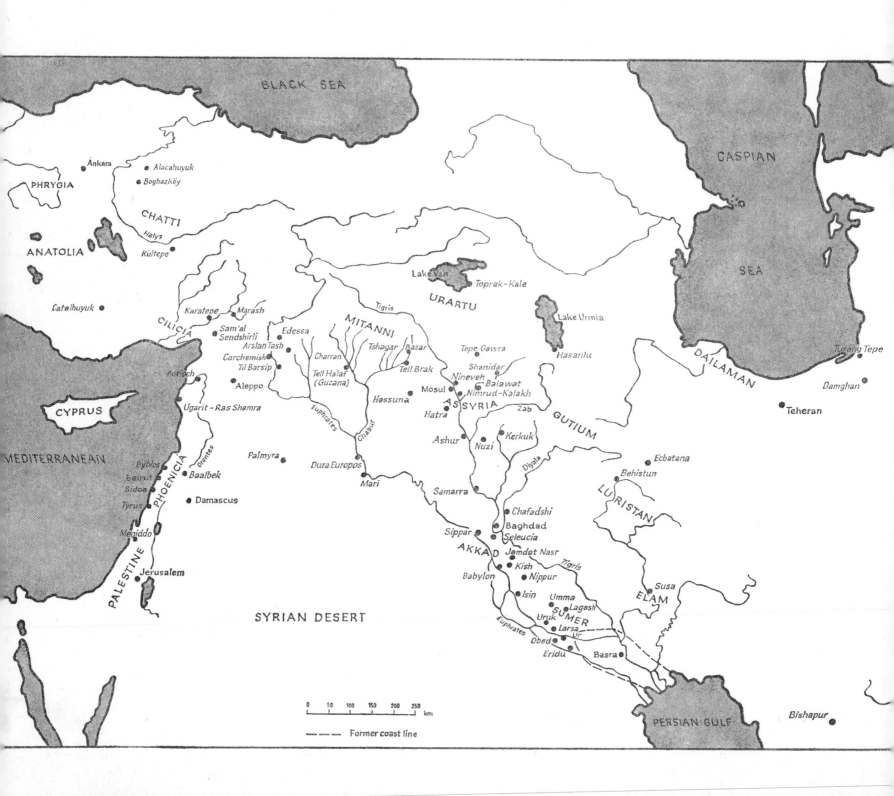

PREFACE

A kind of magic has always surrounded "The East." Every child knows the fairy-tales of *A Thousand and One Nights*, and the image of the lovely Sheherezade who is telling them conceals many another matter which is known to us about the Ancient East. Frequently thoughts about oriental women of the Middle Ages or of antiquity conjure up at once the gay life in the harems, where women with flashing eyes, wrapped in gossamer veils, are supposed to be happy to meet proud rulers with equally flashing eyes, and to enjoy with them a life devoted to flirtation, free of any cares. One imagines— often against one's better judgement— the women in the East spending all their lives filled with the beauty and the ease shown by our popular musical comedies; these and nursery fairy-tales certainly contributed most in producing this picture. But the world conjured up by them is only a fairy-tale world, a beautiful illusion; it certainly ought not to be generalized, either for the Islamic Middle Ages or for the Ancient East. The everyday life of the vast majority of oriental women in ancient times hardly ever seems to have been fairy-tale-like and, therefore, the book we present here is not a pleasant book of fairy-tales. It is rather a report of facts, for as much as possible of what historical sources had to say about the life of women in ancient times, has been collected in these pages.

The era which we want to consider is a large one. The earliest sources referred to belong to the 9th millennium B.C., and the book concludes with reports from the 7th century A.D., that is, from the end of the Sassanid empire. Of the periods surveyed preference has been given to the more ancient oriental ones, to the historical periods leading up to the time of Alexander the Great.

Of course such an extensive theme cannot be treated exhaustively; therefore, a survey is provided instead which includes what is typical, although it also shows many an interesting particularity of women's life; often it is the ancient sources themselves which are made to speak. Owing to the rules which guided this restricted choice, many items worth reporting had to be omitted.

At this point we should like to thank the ladies and gentlemen who have furthered the writing of this book, by their kind suggestions and stimulating advice or by placing photographs at our disposal. Special thanks are due to B. Brentjes and H. Mode, Halle; J. Klima, Prague; and M. Müller, Leipzig.

INTRODUCTION

"Lift your veil, tear it up
And throw it under the tombstone ...
It is not disgraceful to go with the tide of the time.
Remove the veil from your face
And throw it into the fire under the pot ..."

This is a quotation from a poem by the Iraqi poet Basiem-Al-Thuaib, written in 1926. (39)* He hoped to arouse women with his verses and to encourage them to discard the veil, the symbol of their subordination, and to free themselves from their thousands of years of dependence.

The veil, light though it is, has been made burdensome by a variety of symbols, and that not only, as is generally presumed, since the time of Mohammed, but already in the Ancient East; all through this time it has been used as a significant necessity by women, not—or not only— as a flattering accessory to female fashions, but as evidence of their increasing isolation and subordination. A long history is attached to the gossamer light bridal veil, which still today adorns the head of the young bride in many parts of the world, though for the wedding day only. Many a modern young bride might be set musing when she realizes the totally different conditions under which the brides in the Ancient East covered their heads, and still today have to do so. The symbolic act of covering the head was for the brides of the Ancient East very often the beginning of a permanent, and permanently renewed, subordination to their husbands. The oriental wife had to adapt herself to live with her husband's concubines, had to obey him, to serve him. Even now these ancient customs have not completely vanished; nor is it unusual for the bridegroom—and what is more, also among the educated and intellectual classes—to pay to the bride's family a "bride's price" before the wedding.

Compared to the customary law, traditional until then, in the Near East, Mohammed introduced some improvement and relaxation, but as, owing to their religious nature, the rules of the Koran were, and still are, regarded by the faithful Muslim as sacred and inviolable, many a rule, which originally spelt progress, became a rigid bond. Thus sura 4.34 of the Koran is still today thought valid by the orthodox: "Men stand higher than women,

* The numbers put in brackets refer to the Bibliography
page 63 seq.

because God (Allah) has favoured them more than the latter and also because of the expenses, which the men have to incur to provide dowry for the bride. Righteous women are humbly devoted to God ... Should you have to fear that any women may rebel, admonish them, avoid them in the marriage bed and beat them ..." (Paret, R., Der Koran, Stuttgart 1962)

Even nowadays there are still trends which fight modern oriental women's endeavours to gain independence. Conservative poets with their verses fight against the liberation of women:

"They want to unveil the faces of chaste women ...
Verily, I reject progress, if it means unveiling noble women ..."
This is said in a poem by Husein-Al-Dhuraifi. (39)

Yet the modern East frees itself more and more from obsolete customs of the past. Large numbers of women have discarded not only the veil, which covered the face, but also the 'abā'a, the black, coat-like wrap, which covered them from head to toe, thus stepping out of their enforced seclusion. The countries where the most ancient civilizations of mankind once grew and flourished, now increasingly offer women a more dignified place. Women started to study at universities, but it was only in 1938 that an Iraqi woman doctor could begin practising. This example shows clearly that the modern oriental woman is still confronted by problems and difficulties.

Yet we know that the history of all that exists goes back to the past where it has been able to establish its roots and has been moulded by it.

It has, however, to be stated that, although woman in the Ancient East was not given the freedom and the equal rights which ought to have been hers in the family and in society, the ancient history of the Orient as a whole is a glorious one; its achievements during the periods considered in this book have, no doubt, also influenced and helped to form our own civilization. And certainly, women took a large share in this development of the culture of the Ancient East. It is, therefore, only fair to try to re-build their image with the help of the ancient sources and to appreciate their importance.

There are at our disposal many details, enabling us to reconstruct and to illustrate women's life: for approximately a hundred years archaeology has worked untiringly to reveal more and more of the past. Old writings have been deciphered so that now plenty of texts "speak" to us; representations of women from about the 9th millennium B.C. onwards have been saved from the ruins by archaeologists; and since the early 3rd millennium, written testimonies begin in ever increasing numbers.

Several collections of legal texts were among those discovered in the Near East, the most important the *Codex Hammurabi*. With its 282 paragraphs it is more comprehensive and better known than any other collection of the laws of antiquity. Hammurabi was one of the great rulers of the Ancient East, the sixth king of the First Dynasty of Babylon; towards the end of his reign (1728–1686 B.C.), he ordered the laws to be fixed in writing and carved in Akkadian cuneiform letters on a diorite stela of 2.25 m height, which is now in the Louvre.

Altogether it was characteristic of the rulers of the Ancient East to try to "regulate" all relationships in the family as well as in society as a whole. Already before Hammurabi some of the kings issued laws; the honour to have been the first law giver of the world is to be attributed to King Urnammu, who reigned approximately in 2050 B.C. in Ur, a town in the southern part of Mesopotamia *(Codex Urnammu)*. The *Codex Lipit-Ishtar* and the Akkadian laws of Eshnunna also precede in time the *Codex Hammurabi*. From more recent times, the 12th century B.C., dates a codex of Central Assyria. Table A of it has been called *Women's Mirror* (Ill. 53) as its fifty-nine paragraphs deal above all with matters concerning women, a mine of information for the present specialized research. Mention has further to be made of the Neo-Babylonian legal code of the 1st millennium B.C., as well as of the collection of laws of the Hittites, a people in Asia Minor, which has come down to us from the 2nd millennium B.C. In contrast to Egypt, where until now no codices of law have been found, the situation with regard to legal sources is especially auspicious in the Near East. Moreover, we can also make use of a large number of various official documents concerning for example marriage, divorce, dowry, adoption, etc. There are, furthermore, extant private letters, documents from temples and palaces referring to economic matters, dealing, for instance, with the employment and maintenance of workers, etc., and also myths, legends and so on to inform us about the life of earthly women. And lastly there should be mentioned the picturesque and amusing proverbs commenting upon the everyday life of the people in the Ancient East, often divulging "where the shoe pinched them." Some of these proverbs are written in the so-called Emesal dialect, a "women's form of speech", part of the Sumerian language; we may, therefore, assume that they are utterances by women, and this frequently offers us additional information.

The sources are so numerous and so varied that they cannot all be specified. We ought, however, not to neglect to point out that not alone today, but already in Antiquity, countries of the Ancient East have fascinated their neighbours. Herodotus, for example, has reported many an interesting item about the women of the Ancient Orient, and others have followed in his steps. Thus, the life and activities of women are often shown and discussed in ancient sources. Although the modern observer is separated from these eras by whole worlds, yet he is linked to them by many a similarity of historical development. From a historical point of view, Orient and Occident are no contrasts any more, but are joined very closely together.

WOMAN AS MIRRORED IN THE TABLES OF LAW

Anyone taking up a book on the woman and especially one on women in the Ancient East, will expect to find something about Eve, the Biblical "Mother of all living," the famous and infamous companion and partner of Adam. For the "Problem Woman" began—so it is said—with her. Not only is it she who is supposed to have started the history of mankind by her mere existence and by corrupting Adam, but it is also she who has been blamed for everything of which women have ever been accused, whether for good or ill.

However, much may have been written, sung or put into verse about this, according to the Bible Eve's main function was to be the "Mother of all living." She stands before us as one of the numerous mothers of the Ancient East, and as such forms a link in the long chain of ancient oriental mother deities. For us she is not—or no longer—a goddess, but if rightly understood, a "symbol." The manner of her creation symbolizes the close connection, the unity of man and woman. But the conception of Eve leads us to the deified "Great Mother" of the Ancient East, whose worship and prestige point to a somewhat similar position of women in the then contemporary society. Eve herself thus provides us with information about her own historical period, and as one of the best-known legendary women of Antiquity, she ought not to be omitted from our review.

Moreover, some of her characteristics show clearly her connection with the original myths of the Ancient East. There is even a manifest link with Sumerian legends, in which a "rib" and the "female ruler of life" play a part. These few lines, which we devote here at the beginning of this chapter to the famous Eve, constitute no digression but a straight path to the earliest sources revealing something about the legal position of women, with which we now have to begin our survey. It was the well-known American scholar S. N. Kramer, who discovered the connection between the Eve of the Bible and Sumerian mythology. (58) The Sumerians knew a paradise with four rivers, including Euphrates and Tigris, which closely resembled the Garden of Eden; according to a legend the great mother goddess Ninchursag allowed eight lovely plants to sprout in this garden. Enki, the water god, ate from them, although this was forbidden; and Ninchursag, angry about it, though not expelling him from the garden, yet condemned him to death. He fell ill, eight of his organs were affected and his strength

Couple of lovers in close embrace

failed him. Only a sly fox was able to induce the wrathful Ninchursag to save Enki from death. She then enquired about his suffering and created one special healing deity for each of his sick organs. Here follows a very interesting passage in the legend, which, according to Kramer, takes us back to the Biblical Eve. One of the eight questions was:

"My brother, what hurts you?"

"My rib hurts me."

"To the goddess Ninti I have given birth for you." "Ninti" however has a double meaning in the Sumerian language: "female ruler of the rib" and "female ruler of life," as "ti" means "rib" as well as "create life." In Hebrew the name "Eve" means approximately "she who creates life," "mother of all living." According to Kramer one can therefore draw a straight line, connecting the Sumerian goddess Ninti—female ruler of the rib and of life—to the Eve of the Bible. We ought further to state that the "mother," the "ruler of life" occupied a permanent and important place in the religions of the entire Ancient East, although she appeared in the different areas and at various epochs in dissimilar forms. The "mother" was, especially in prehistoric times, the central figure of religious conceptions. Images found of her were worshipped as those of a deity; they have been discovered in large numbers in many a place (Ill. 1, 2, 3). Such statuettes of the "Great Mother" have been excavated also in the area of Palestine, where the Biblical story of paradise and of Adam and Eve was written down. Thousands of years ago mankind's thoughts revolved around "she who creates life," around the mother, the woman.

This outstanding importance of the mother, worshipped as a deity, is meaningful for us also with regard to the legal position of women in the relevant epochs. The dominating mother-cults could be established only because of the great esteem in which woman was held as the bearer of life, the mother of the family, the head of the tribe, the priestess, the ancestress. This esteem is shown for instance in the careful burials of women, supplied with valuable offerings, which were arranged for them even in temples and other sites dedicated to religious observances. James Mellaart, who led the excavations at Catalhuyuk in Asia Minor, has ascertained that only women were granted such dignified burials; corresponding burials for men have so far not been found in the sanctuaries (Ill. 4). (79) This shows that in very early times, with no class-like social distinctions, the position of women was a very favourable, even privileged one. On the other hand, it has to be pointed out that the Eve of the Old Testament had to submit to the authority of the male, as she was told to "serve him." The common life of the first human couple was, therefore, already organized according to patriarchal rules, a proof for the comparatively "young" age of the story of paradise; with the progress of social development and the emergence of differentiated social conditions, man had taken a more and more prominent position. Firmly established families, under the patriarchal leadership of the man, made up the individual picture, while the recently established city-states or temple-states with a priest-prince as their head, became characteristic of the whole social organization. This forms in the early 3rd millennium B.C. a clearly delineated picture. Considerable social differences become obvious from the wide range of archaeological discoveries in the Ancient East, in particular in Uruk and Elam, and these social differences also affected the masses of the female population. On the one hand the women of the early 3rd millennium held the highest offices as priestesses and gained, thereby, no small measure of influence and power (Ill. 6), while on the other hand members of the same sex had to serve as slaves in the temples.

At the same time this so-called "Uruk period" represents the climax of the Sumerian civilization; it not only left to posterity magnificent monumental and small-sized works of art, but also such inventions as the cylinder seal and the art of writing. Women joined this rapid cultural progress as an integral part, some of them as simple manual workers, some as craftswomen, and not a few of them in leading positions, for example in the organization of the cult; they thus joined the various classes of the recently progressing and much diversified society.

This progress continued in the following centuries, though not everywhere without interruptions and not quite alike everywhere. To begin with, the sources of the 3rd millennium B.C. offer us but scanty material which, however, is particularly interesting. This applies first of all to finds in the royal graves at Ur, dating from the mid-third millennium, the so-called Early Dynastic period. The excavators discovered that when one of the rulers of this period died, all his retinue was killed and buried with him, probably after having been doped with some drug. Even complete teams with oxen and their drivers were buried. In one case there were about seventy women among those buried with the king, all placed with precious jewellery and partly with their musical instruments quite near to the ruler (Ill. 11). A female ruler or priestess, too, was granted a similar burial. Much has been surmised and written about these finds (83), but they are still not unequivocally explained. They seem to be characteristic of a certain phase of historic development with recently differentiated social classes, as similar discoveries have been made at Kish in Mesopotamia, in Egypt, China and Mycenae. These burials, however, cannot provide a general information with regard to the place of woman in the family. Yet that much seems to be evident: the rulers of these early city-states possessed the power over life and death of their subjects. But it is hardly possible to imagine how these huge privileges of the rulers affected the individuals. Attempts at reforms by individual rulers, such as Urukagina of Lagash (approximately 2355 B.C.), aimed at easing life for the poor, the "widow and the orphan;" at abolishing exploitation and arbitrariness and at re-establishing "freedom," mentioned here for the first time. They indicate very unsatisfactory social conditions. On the other hand, it is interesting that women until then had retained the traditional "right" to polyandry, a relic among others of earlier epochs that was done away with by Urukagina.

The 3rd millennium was, therefore, in Mesopotamia, still characterized by remains of past epochs. As to the sources from which to draw a picture of woman's position in the family, we still find them insufficient; the number of texts with information for our theme increased only at the turn to the 2nd millennium. From that period date collections of laws, marriage contracts, documents from law courts, etc.; these are important evidence by which we gain insight into many of the spheres of women's daily life.

Later on we shall describe the status of the woman in society, her work and her numerous activities in economic life: at first, however, we shall examine her position in the family, her legal rights inside this narrower sphere; this will help us eventually to understand the part she played in the wider range of society.

It is of interest to note what a favourable position the women occupied and retained under the supremacy of the man in the early oriental society, a society which was organized in differentiated classes, long before anything of the kind developed in Europe. Notwithstanding the patriarchal rights of man, woman seems to have secured for herself at first a fair amount of independence. It is for instance remarkable and gratifying to see many a document of the late Sumerian time (approximately 2000 B.C.), distinguished from any later one by reporting on the unconcerned and unafraid attitude of women when appearing in court.

Although at marriage the woman of the Ancient East was always only an "object" given by her parents into matrimony and then "taken" by her husband, yet she could at that time dare to deny herself to her husband and to forbid him to put "his head" near her "bonnet," without incurring punishment for it. (21, No. 26) At the period of Hammurabi, on the other hand, to deny the consummation of marriage was considered a punishable crime for the wife who, if she had not behaved well besides, was threatened with death by being thrown into water (CH paragraphs 142 seq.). Moreover, it seems as if the dissolution of marriage had not been so difficult for her in the more recent Sumerian period as in that of Hammurabi (21, No. 169, she has "renounced her rights as a married wife"). The Sumerian woman was, therefore, in a rather favourable position; this applies also to the female slave, as we shall see at the end of this chapter. But these "relative" differences did not alter the fact that in the Ancient East matrimony was basically organized on patriarchal rules. The husband was acknowledged always and everywhere the undisputed head of the family, and his wife, as well as his concubines, his sons and daughters, all had to show him due respect. A text from the middle of the 3rd millennium states that if a wife contradicts him, her teeth ought to be smashed with burnt bricks. (60, p. 322) As head of the family the man was the lord, in fact the owner of his wife and his children, although his ownership did not entitle him to kill them without reason. But if he caught his wife in adultery he had the right to kill her. (Heth 1 paragraph 197; MAss paragraph 15). In the most diverse ways the wives were in the husband's power. They were liable for any violation of law by him and there are proofs that to honour a debt, he could pawn or sell his wife, son or daughter as if they were objects. Those pawned, usually the wife or the daughter, had to serve in the house of the creditor or buyer, and their fate often was very hard, as it seems as if they were frequently exploited as much as possible (MAss paragraph 44). (89, p. 91) Hammurabi's decrees explicitly forbid the beating or oppressing of these "pawns" and they also limited the pawning to three years (CH paragraphs 116, 117). Later, however, in the mid-Assyrian period (approx. 12th century B.C.) other law givers omitted these protective measures from the so-called *Woman's Mirror*. Permission is even explicitly given to beat a "pawn" if it had been accepted for the full price, to pull it by the hair and to pierce its ears (paragraph 44); thus the safeguards which Hammurabi's laws had provided for the women were evidently reduced in the mid-Assyrian epoch. A document of this period concerning the sale of a wife for an unlimited time fits into this usage. The contract for this sale states: "Bēl-qarrad ... son of Shamash- ... has handed over Mārat-Ishtar, the daughter of Papsukkal-saduni, his wife, for the full price to Kidin-Adad, the son of Iddin-Kube. She is bought and taken. Bēl-qarrad has received the lead as price for his wife. Bēl-qarrad is liable for the extradition of his wife." (113) The woman in question was not a concubine or slave, but quite evidently the legitimate wife, a free woman, as the name of her father is mentioned, which was done only in the case of free persons. Unfortunately no reasons are given for this barbarous sale. Whether the husband sold her from necessity or as punishment for proved unfaithfulness (this too could have been the reason): he certainly was in principle entitled to sell his wife. At the time of the Sassanids the husband had even the right to "lend" his wife, as stated in the law codex: "... to lend his principal wife to another man, who is in need of a woman for his children, is not himself responsible for this need, and has asked for the woman in the proper manner. She can be loaned even without her consent being asked, and when that has been done, her chattels do not go to the man to whom she is given." (5, p. 14)

Other privileges of the husband are particularly manifest with regard to divorce. The husband encountered no special difficulties when he wanted to get rid of his wife, especially if she had not borne him any children. He only had to pay a fine in money ("divorce money") and to return the dowry she had brought him. But for the wife it was thought something abominable to ask for a divorce. By her marriage she had been turned into part of her husband's "possessions," as he usually had paid the "bride's money" to her parents—originally a kind of purchase price. The wife could anull this arrangement of ownership only under exceptional circumstances when there were some weighty reasons, for instance when the husband had repeatedly wounded her feelings in an unbearable way and if a public inquiry "at the gates" had confirmed her innocence (CH paragraph 142). Otherwise, she had to expect harsh punishment, slavery, to be sold out of the house, even death by being thrown into the water or from the tower. Frequently this was stipulated in writing already in the marriage contract. It seems, however, likely that, gradually, a more tolerant judgement could be established; women, too, only had to pay a fine for divorce. Yet it has to be stated that there seems to have been no rules for this; evidently each of the partners bargained for the best conditions to be entered in the contract. Social standing and economic importance certainly played a part. Thus it happened that from one and the same period—for example the reign of Samsuiluna, the son of Hammurabi,—some very different documents have been preserved: the marriage contract of the priest Enlil-issu (1737 B.C.) conceded to him as well as to his wife Amasukkal the same conditions for divorce: half a *mina* of silver (54, No. 777), while the contemporary marriage contract of a certain Rīmum stipulates ten *shekel* of silver as a fine for him but, for his wife Bāshtum death by drowning. (51, p. 195) It is, however, not known how often one really resorted to the death sentence for the request of divorce by the wife; frequently the stipulation of harsh punishment might have been used only as a deterrent. Nevertheless, for a woman to demand divorce was generally thought to be scandalous and indecent, deserving punishment. A report from Nuzi, as recent as from the middle of the 2nd millennium, tells us that her garments were torn off her body and she herself chased ignominiously out of the house. (104, No. 19) Yet as threats of punishment for the wife were not entered any more into many marriage contracts, one may assume that a greater tolerance was generally accepted.

It is interesting that divorce took place also in royal families, and was treated there according to the generally prevalent custom. A process of this kind has been preserved from Ugarit. Had there then already been any newspapers, this "scandal" would have provided headlines. As it was, it produced much excitement which can still be guessed at from the documents. King Ammistamru II of Ugarit (approx. 1250 B.C.) had married a daughter of Benteshina, the king of Amurru; he had several children by her. It is reported, however, that "she gave only headaches" to Ammistamru. The king divorced her, and his supreme sovereign, the Hittite Great-King Tudhaliyas IV and King Ini-Teshup of Carchemish confirmed the divorce by a decree, laying down that the dowry had to be returned to the divorced woman. The position of the crown-prince regarding the succession to the throne was then of course politically important; it was left to him to decide whether or not he wanted to follow his mother. If he took sides with her he had to "lay his garments on the throne" and was excluded from the succession. (The crown-prince seems to have chosen this way, as nothing has been discovered of any reign of his.) The divorced queen was compelled to waive any claims on her other sons, daughters or sons-in-law, for, so it was stated, "they belong to Ammistamru, the king of Ugarit." (88) This royal divorce tells us how the problem of "dowry" and "children" used to be settled: the husband who had to return the dowry, was, however, on the other hand entitled to claim the children. But exceptions either way are known; for instance CH paragraph 137 reports that divorced priestesses could retain their dowries and half of their other possessions, with which to educate their children, who evidently were also left to them. An old-Assyrian document even mentions leaving both the children and all the money and other chattels to the woman. (51, p. 190) Quite different from these arrangements so favourable for the wife, is the custom of the mid-Assyrian period (second half of 2nd millennium B.C.). There the divorced wife appears to have been completely at the husband's mercy. Paragraph 37 of the *Woman's Mirror* says: "When a husband leaves his wife, he will give her something if his heart so desires; if he does not desire it, he will not give her anything; she will leave empty-handed." Others could be added to these examples. They show us the diversity of the problem and warn us not to generalize by using anyone of them alone. It seems, however, as if the position of women had been particularly unpleasant in the mid-Assyrian period.

As the wife's intention to divorce was thought to be an encroachment on the "family," on the patriarchal rights of the man, her adultery was of course considered a far worse crime. Adultery was punished most severely—*nota bene*, only when committed by the wife. In none of the collections of laws is there any indication that the idea jo the infidelity of the husband was at all known. In fact, this would have been very confusing, as the generally acknowledged form of marriage gave the husband the right to have a principal wife, a concubine and slaves "for his desires," so as to make sure of having descendants, if even only through a "girl from a brothel." In any case, adultery was known as a fact only with regard to the wife.

The laws of Eshnunna (2nd millennium B.C.) already state: "On the day on which she is found in a citizen's lap, she is to die, she no longer lives." In all the Near East this crime was deemed to deserve death for the wife herself and for her "paramour" and there was no change as to this for centuries. Neo-Babylonian marriage contracts of the 6th century B.C. still stipulate for the wife's adultery: "She shall die through the iron dagger" or "she shall die by being beaten to death." (98, p. 3; 75, p. 3) Of course sympathy and love may have mitigated many a punishment. The differentiated legal position of husband and wife does not exclude love and respect. The legislator sometimes even reckons with it: "If the husband brings his adulterous wife to the gates of the palace and says: 'My wife does not die,' then he saves her life and saves also the paramour." This is stated in paragraph 198 of the Hittite laws, and similar passages are to be found in the laws of Hammurabi and of mid-Assyrian ones (paragraphs 129 and 15). Yet the sinners evidently did not always escape the punishment of death. There is a protocol of testimonies from Lagash in a process about libel, which followed an awkward "group-sex affair" and the break up of a marriage (approximately 2000 B.C.). It reads: "... you will swear several times by Ningishzida 'Bēlshunu has not known me ...' I, myself, am convinced that he ... regularly sleeps with you. You have agreed with Bēlshunu what to say ... If you do not want to die, convince me that what I say is untrue!" (free translation of 70, p. 46)

The death sentence probably also threatened an adulteress (?) who had fled and of whom to get hold of again Ammistamru II of Ugarit tried every means he could think of. (85, p. 280 seq.) No name is given for the "great lady's daughter," the fugitive in question, who is supposed to have committed this "great sin;" nor do we know whether this affair is connected with the divorce already mentioned. At any rate Ammistamru tried stubbornly to find her even with an unsuccessful military attack and eventually with the help of a decree from his overlord, His Majesty the Hittite Great-King. For her surrender he paid a fortune, 1400 *shekel* in gold. But unfortunately this is all that the documents disclose, although news about the punishment would have been interesting, particularly as there is seldom evidence about the actual punishment of the woman, though this would have been helpful in appreciating her legal situation. Evidently it was often possible to substitute fines for corporal punishment; in the *Woman's Mirror* (paragraph 24), for example, the husband is offered the choice to have the ears of his condemned wife cut off or to redeem the sinner with money. According to the report on a process in Nuzi, in which a female slave was condemned, her master seems to have chosen the "cheaper way," the cutting off of a finger, instead of the fine of a number of cattle. (32)

One could enumerate many more items to illustrate the difference in the valuation of man and woman, for instance the fact that daughters were placed at a disadvantage compared to sons with regard to inheritance, etc. It is, however, unfortunately impossible to give an exhaustive report of all the relevant facts. But it must be mentioned that, owing to the particular build-up of the families, even women living together in one family did not enjoy equal rights. The marriage of the Ancient East was supposed to be monogamic as the man usually had only one principal wife, but as is well-known he could take a concubine, especially when his wife had not borne him any children. It was even the duty of the childless wife to procure a concubine for him, so that he might have children. Female slaves, too, were at the disposal of their master and therefore the legislators had to provide a number of regulations concerning the problem of the principal wife, concubine and slave, as all these women living together were bound to create various difficulties. The principal wife was the mistress of the house, and she was most anxious that her authority be not impaired and that neither the concubine nor a favoured slave should overstep the limits set to them. These women had to expect unsparing punishment if they tried to put themselves on an equal footing with her: they could be degraded, even sold out of the house. Harsh corporal punishments

were also provided, as can be gathered from the recently deciphered fragment of a legal codex (probably part of the *Codex Urnammu* of approx. 2050 B.C.): "If a female slave tries to put herself on the same footing as her mistress and utters a curse against her, one *sila* of salt (= 0.404 l) will be rubbed into her teeth." (56) Some marriage contracts clearly delineated the hierarchy and the duties of the principal wife and the concubine. The following contract has been preserved from the 18th century B.C.:

"Warad Shamash has taken Tarām-Sagila and Iltani, the daughter of Sin-abushu, as his wives. If Tarām-Sagila or Iltani said to Warad-Shamash, their husband, 'you are not my husband,' she will be thrown from the tower. And when Warad-Shamash says to Tarām-Sagila or to Iltani, his wives, 'you are not my wife,' he will forfeit his house and chattels. Iltani will wash the feet of Tarām-Sagila and carry her chair to the house of her god. If Tarām-Sagila is angry, Iltani, too, will be angry; if she is gay, she, too, will be gay. She will not break her seal. She will grind and bake for her ten *qa* of flour." (Signed by ten witnesses.)

(54, No. 2)

Warad-Shamash evidently married together with his principal wife a concubine, who then occupied a lower rank and had to serve the principal wife. Possibly the principal wife was a priestess who was bound to remain childless. For cases like this the *Codex Hammurabi* specially permitted marriage with another, lower-rank priestess or the taking of a slave, so as to make sure of the desired number of children. Generally the woman with children was more esteemed and granted better protection by law than the childless woman; and among the mothers those were more esteemed who had borne sons. Thus a small slab from Persepolis (504 B.C.) tells us about the supply of wine to seven women who had borne sons; each of them was given one flask, while ten women who had borne daughters were given only half a flask each. (46, p. 86) And anyway a wife with children occupied a better legal position with regard to her husband. He had to expect a considerable financial loss if he wanted to divorce her and this might have induced him under certain circumstances to think twice about his original plan of a divorce. The female slave who had borne children to her master, was likewise in a better position than a childless one: she could not be sold out of the house and after her master's death she could, together with her children, gain freedom; if recognized by the father, her children had even the right of inheritance (CH paragraphs 170, 171).

As we have already mentioned, the woman of the Ancient East was not an outlawed person, excluded from social life. Although more or less restricted by the laws serving mainly the upper classes and by the public order established by them, yet she had also, on the basis of the patriarchal family organization, various means of taking an active part in public life and of occupying an important place in the community.

Naturally the role played in public life by the wife was smaller than that of the husband, as her activities were mainly concentrated on the family, the upbringing of children and the household. She is, however, mentioned in numerous documents and has left behind her a large number of reports of her energy and her activity in the most varied spheres. She evidently made good use of all chances offered to her and was no less clever and efficient than any other woman at any other time. Already the early reports on palaces and temples of the 3rd millennium show in their lists the work done by women in various trades and other occupations: as potters, weavers, spinners, hairdressers, as agricultural workers, in breweries, kitchens, bakeries, etc. Their wages were paid in kind and usually were lower than those of the men. Women also showed themselves able to fill elevated positions, for example, as rulers, governors or priestesses (Ill. 6, 62). In the course of centuries their abilities became more varied and specialized, their handicraft developed, their knowledge expanded. They practised professions which demanded long and complicated training, as for instance that of the scribe. We are told by a Sumerian document concerning schools that a scribe had to attend the scribes' school "from boyhood to manhood." Evidently girls, too, had for many years to go to school until they could manage the complicated art of reading and writing. From the 3rd millennium a few female scribes have become known to us, later quite a number, some of them even by their names. A midwife, too, seems to have been given a certain training or education. She is called the "woman who knows the inside." Images and texts show and mention many more activities of women: there were famous singers, who could present their singing and reciting with great art (Ill. 5). Their singing was

accompanied by instrumental music, in which not men alone, but also women were experts. In the tombs at Ur, precious lyres with beautiful inlaid work have been found with the women buried there. Female singers were employed mainly in the palaces and temples, and specially experienced artists there also trained their successors according to plan. A passage in one of the texts mentions that "the female singers settled down to learn." (111, p. 31) Certainly they, too, had to dedicate considerable time to the study of singing and recitation, the playing of instruments and dancing. The number of the female singers evidently was very high: at a temple in Nippur there was even in the mid-2nd millennium B.C. a "clinic" where the male and female singers, who had come there partly from abroad, could be treated when they fell ill; their complaints and ailments consisted mainly in coughs, colic, fever, etc. They were very well cared for, and the head of the clinic reported daily to a high official on the health of the patients and the methods of their treatment. Thus, qualified singers seem to have been highly esteemed.

This, however, does not apply to another occupation of women frequently to be found in the Ancient East—that of the female publican. Its representatives often got into conflict with law and had to be reprimanded and called to order, chiefly for rigging prices, fraudulence, deceiving or other crimes deserving the punishment of death. These "beer-women" evidently were very sturdy ladies; one of them, an innkeeper called Kubaba, even succeeded in approximately 2500 B.C. in ascending the king's throne and becoming one of the few independently reigning queens of the Ancient East.

In any case, all this points to the fact that, in principle, women could ply any trade on their own, some of them quite unusual, but historically interesting, like that of the "dream interpreter" or of the "collector of salt." Emphasis has also to be laid on the fact that the earliest "chemists" known to us by name were two Mesopotamian women of the 13th century B.C. (Journal of Chemical Education, 32, 1955, p. 182). Women were therefore to be found in the most varied employment and contributed steadily to economic and social development. Moreover, they enjoyed considerable civic rights: in a court of divorce of 1727 B.C. in Nippur the decision was not, as was the custom, to be made by the "elders," that is male officials of the law court, but by a female group especially appointed to the court for this special case. (38; 70) Apart from these official duties women were entitled to carry on the business of law concerning their own affairs and also to act as witnesses. They could buy and sell (also slaves), take on lease, rent and let, adopt, though probably not in Ugarit (86), etc. To seal documents, they frequently used a seal of their own. These were, as far as we know, rights due to all free women. But often, when married wives concluded any legal business, the husband had to be present, wherefrom one may conclude that his consent was needed (perhaps mainly when it concerned their common possessions and the like). Many documents and contracts refer, however, only to the wife, not to her husband; this is, for instance, clearly shown in some Neo-Babylonian documents or in those of Tulpunnaya from Nuzi (15th century B.C.).

There was, furthermore, one group of women who were particularly active in legal matters and are bound to have played a not too small role in the economic and social life of their town: the priestesses. There were many kinds of priestesses, as can be gathered from the various names given to this rank. In old-Babylonian documents alone there are mentioned, for example the "entum," the "nadiātum," the "shugītum," the "zikrum," the "qadishtum," the "ishtarītum" and the "kulmashītum." (92) Also in various other parts of the Ancient East the profession of the priestesses was more or less specialized. It is, however, usually impossible to determine exactly the individual functions as it is mostly difficult, if not impossible, to translate the words indicating them. But about some of the priestesses or servants of the gods we are well informed, for instance about the nadiātum, of whom much of interest has become known. Although nothing is known as yet (41) of any special religious activities by these women, they are usually called priestesses, a term which here has a wider and more comprehensive meaning. The nadiātum were not chosen by their god with the help of a "liver-omen," as was done for high-priestesses, but probably were dedicated to him already in childhood by their fathers. That this took place in early childhood seems indicated by the procedure being called "lifting up to the god" (CH paragraph 181). Interesting is the fact that the nadiātum lived together in a "secluded house," the *gagūm*, which can be translated as convent or convent-like institution; several such

"convents" have become known from ancient Babylonian times, for example in Kish, Nippur, Larsa and other places. (The best known, largest and that from which the greatest number of documents is extant, is the *gagūm* in Sippar, dedicated to the god Shamash.) It has been calculated that at the time of Hammurabi not less than one hundred and forty nadiātum lived there together; before and after that time their number was smaller. It evidently was thought important that the life of these priestesses should be irreproachable, otherwise one would not have given them several (usually three) supervisors. Besides there were their janitors and several other male officials, such as judges and scribes. But there were also female "officials," several female wardens and scribes, some of whom are named again and again in the documents, so that one may assume that they occupied these posts for a long time (the scribe Amat-Mamu for at least forty years). The head-warden used to be a male sangu-priest.

Nevertheless, the rules of these convents were not too strict: most of the nadiātum lived inside the convent walls in houses of their own and were given time to attend to all kinds of business, and for visits in and out of town. Numerous documents prove that the nadiātum were good business women to whose enterprising minds we owe many a vivid report on legal, economic and other matters of cultural importance. It is evident that they exercised a decisive influence on the economic life of their town. For example it has been ascertained that proportionally there were fewer merchants in the town of Sippar than in that of Larsa, probably because in Sippar it was the nadiātum who played the vital role in business with their transactions. (76) The importance of these women in economic life was therefore rather valuable. One has, however, to remember that this applied to a privileged group of women, who right from their childhood had been supported with special rights by the legislator. The nadiātum could freely dispose of the dowry which her father gave her (CH paragraph 179), and as to inheritance she was in a better position than most other women, as she could inherit like a "hereditary son." In matrimony, too, and in the court of divorce, the law favoured her; but marriages of nadiātum were rare, though in principle they were not forbidden. This is all the more surprising, as they were not allowed to have children, their marriage thereby being senseless according to the ancient oriental concept of matrimony. Moreover, one would conclude from their name—"nadītum" means "fallow"—that they were not meant to marry, had the contrary not been proved by the sources. The *Codex Hammurabi* dedicates several paragraphs to marriages of this kind (paragraphs 137, 144–147), with special regard to the position of the concubine, the "substitute woman" who was to bear the children of the man. Of the more than six hundred nadiātum of the god Shamash in Sippar, known to us by name, none was married, while among the seventeen nadiātum of the god Marduk there were seven married women, of whom four had brought their own sisters as concubines, so as to secure posterity.

The documents show that many of the nadiātum came from "high society", that is, the families of high officials, some even from the royal dynasty. It has been assumed that it was one of the main concerns of fathers to give their daughters away to "convents," as their possessions returned to the father's family at their death, except when special provision had been made to prevent this (CH paragraph 179). The nadiātum on their part were able to conclude lucrative bargains: they leased and let houses, fields, gardens, acquired female slaves, adopted younger nadiātum so that in their own old age they might be nursed and cared for by them; they drew up work contracts for the management of their real estate, gave loans, also loans for corn, etc.

Obviously not every nadītum was in so favoured a position as to own her house; the richer ones made bargains also with those of lesser means. Thus a certain Ribatum increased the rent of her house in a not very fair way from 3 to 5 *shekel*.

As is to be expected, the priestesses, who were members of the royal family, were especially wealthy. The most important of them and most frequently mentioned was Iltani, the daughter of Samsuiluna (or Abi-eshukh). For the administration of her estates she had to have a larger team of officials who also had to organize the employment of harvest workers, etc. She kept six cowherds to look after her 1085 head of cattle. Of course, that was an exception; but on a smaller scale, other nadiātum were occupied in a similar manner. It need not be emphasized that priestesses have been outstanding, not only in the time of the ancient Babylonian kingdoms but also at many other periods and in other districts, where they gave proof of their efficiency to deal with business and legal problems.

It is less well known, and will probably be surprising to learn, that priestesses were also connected with criminal events; yet quite a number of examples could be quoted to show their legal position from another side. Sometimes they were the victims of criminal attacks, sometimes they themselves were the infamous actors. Thus it is reported that a certain Sin-iddinam ill-treated several of the Shamash priestesses in Sippar. When one of the "servants of Shamash" called him to account for not having paid some garment, he cruelly beat her and even bragged that he had beaten not only her but also "five other Shamash ladies." (63, No. 34) Thus, he had done to this Shamash-servant "what does not happen in this country," and what was an outrageous insult, a negative yet telling proof of the priestesses' great prestige. Physical attacks on priestesses, rapes and also "repeated sexual intercourse with the en-priestess" seem not to have been unusual. (92, p. 131)

Among the transgressions of which priests and priestesses were accused, was the theft of treasures from the temples. This obviously happened rather often, so that one partly resorted to queer measures to provide some safeguard. A text from Elam (approximately 1500–1350 B.C.) reports: "As night falls, four female guards have to enter the temple. To make it impossible for them to detach the gold from the statues and to hide it in belts over their privy parts, these are to be tied high up with the help of leather straps." (45, p. 53) To enter a public house was regarded as extremely bad. According to CH paragraph 110 nadiātum and entum priestesses "who opened the door of a beer house" or "went into the beer house for beer" had to expect even the death sentence. It was, however, not the drinking of alcohol that was thought to be deserving of punishment—this was not forbidden to the priestesses, the texts even say that they received rations of beer—it was the visit to the public house which had the reputation of being disreputable and immoral. The reputation of the female publicans, the "beer women," was, as we have already noticed, not a good one. There would still be much more to be said about priestesses, also about those who since the time of Herodotus, at the latest, had been connected with "love" and usually were called "hierodules;" more will be told later about priestesses of this kind.

But to complete what has been said here about priestesses, a few words have to be added about their importance for the Ancient East. For they were very important not only as regards economics, but also concerning political and ideological questions. This applies mainly to the priestesses of exalted rank, most of whom came from the higher layer of the population. Owing to the positions they occupied in the religion of the country they could greatly influence the people. The genealogy of many of these high-priestesses, the "élite" of their profession, is known; for instance, nearly everyone of the high-priestesses of the moon god Nannar in Ur was a member of the royal family, like the famous Encheduanna (probably a daughter of Sargon of Akkad, Ill. 21), or Ennirgalanna (daughter of Urnammu), Enanedu (daughter of Kudurmabuk and simultaneously sister of Rimsin) and many others. Clearly this close connection of temple and palace, customary all over the Ancient East, considerably strengthened the upper layers of society. The king could expect that he would not have to reign with temple and priests as adverseries, but that he could count on their good will and help. It was probably these reasons which induced King Nabonidus many centuries later to revert to this old tradition and to use omens to dedicate his daughter as a high-priestess to the temple service.

No doubt, therefore, the priestesses were able to influence in a far-reaching way the life of society, the economic structure of the country, the development of civilization, and last but not least the mentality of their contemporaries.

It is furthermore necessary to compare the legal and social position of the female slave with that of the free woman, because the former was in many a respect of relatively greater importance to the life of the Ancient East. The ancient sources never indicate that one recognized, much less that one appreciated, the part played by this class of people in the development of the civilization of the Ancient East. Lists concerning the economics of the temples and palaces show that large numbers of female and male slaves were active in all branches of these institutions—the progress and well-being of which would have been impossible without their manual work, skill and abilities. Female slaves were employed in the most varied occupations. We know that skilled female weavers were in demand and greatly valued (65, p. 15), as costly woven materials and fine garments were wanted, not only by the members of the well-to-do groups of the population. They also formed an important item for export. (72, p. 179) In the temple of the moon god at Ur there was a "dress factory" where 98 women and 63 children were employed (MJ 1925). As mentioned before, female slaves worked in "public" institutions like temples and palaces and also in private households and in the family of their master. The value of an efficient slave was well recognized and her price fixed accordingly: "She is a very good-looking slave. Half a *mina* of silver is not too much for her, moreover she is a mother, a weaver and busy day and night." (16, p. 110) (In Hammurabi's time a female slave cost about 20 *shekel*, which was the price of one head of cattle; in the Neo-Babylonian period 50 *shekel*, in the Persian 60–90 *shekel*.) A skilled and experienced slave could, in many a way, be a "treasure" for her master: first of all as a worker and generally as an object which he could sell, lend, pawn, bequeathe, etc. If she had children, these too were his property and increased the number of his slaves; if, besides, she was pretty and attractive, her master could find special pleasure in her and make her his concubine. To attain this he did not grudge money or pains. He gave orders to secure for him for sexual intercourse with her, a "good-looking, fair-skinned" slave (65, p. 60), or an "efficient slave who had given birth already once or twice." (1, No. 20) For a female slave it could be of great importance to win the love of her master by efficiency and beauty and erotic charm, and to bear him children. This gave her the chance to gain freedom for herself and her children (CLI paragraph 25; CH paragraph 171), either by an act of grace already in her master's lifetime or by a legal act after his death. As mother, the position of the slave—as also that of the free woman—was more favourable than that of the childless woman; if, for example, she had fallen into servitude because of debts, she had to be redeemed (CH paragraph 119), and as a rule was also protected against any attempt to sell her again (CH paragraph 146).

This is not the place to give a detailed report on the various sources of slavery. Apart from those born in slavery, prisoners of war have no doubt always formed a large contingent of them (Ill. 67). Some of them came as workers to the palaces or were dedicated to the temples; others were apportioned to private households. There are long lists dating from the late Assyrian period, indicating that large families were particularly appreciated as booty. (17, p. 6 seq.) But one of the largest additions to the number of slaves came from those who were forced into it by poverty. It is known by documents from various periods that free men sold themselves, sometimes also their wives, their children, even their sisters or mothers into slavery, because of destitution or debts. Reports are extant even of women who sold themselves: a certain Wachuluki sold herself and her children as slaves to Tehiptilla, a rich business man from Nuzi (approximately mid-2nd millennium). According to her contract, her and her children's eyes were to be put out, should she rebel against her position as a slave. (81, p. 17)

Especially sad are the sales of children who were torn out of the family, very often to face a hopeless fate in slavery. (21, p. 85; 81, p. 9) The sale of young girls frequently served prostitution, a trade that was lucrative for the "entrepreneur" even in antiquity. In many contracts this purpose of the sale is mentioned quite candidly. A contract of this kind of the time of Rimsin of Larsa (18th century B.C.) reads: "Awirtum shall be made a prostitute, and from her earnings she shall provide for Shallurtum, her mother. If Awirtum should say to Shallurtum, 'you are not my mother,' she shall be sold for money." (81, p. 21)

This contract shows that the sale of this girl (the parents received $1^2/_3$ *shekel* silver) was given the form of an "adoption" which was quite frequent in the Ancient East. The original aim of adoption, to gain, in the case of childlessness, an heir and for old age someone, male or female, as a support, was often —although not always— changed into a "business transaction." Owing to legal contracts of adoption (sale), some of these "adopted" remained all through their lives in the power of their purchaser who could abuse it in any way he chose. Some contracts from Nuzi especially make it quite clear that "adoptions" frequently have to be classified as sales; the corruption of these male or female employers could not have been worse. By various paragraphs in the contracts they secured for themselves far-reaching powers to deal at will with the girls whom they had "adopted as daughters" or "daughters-in-law." If they did not make the girl a prostitute they were anxious to marry her to one of their slaves, so as to increase the members of the new generation of slave children. This could be continued endlessly, as was said: "When ten of her husbands have died, she will be given to an eleventh as his wife."

Owing to these degrading customs, it could, of course, not be prevented when one or the other of the girls should try to find a means of escaping this fate. The language of the documents is reserved, yet between the lines they sometimes show a tragedy which is moving even today after so many centuries. By chance we have several documents concerning a slave called Kisaya, which give us a fair amount of more exact information about this particular girl's fate. Kisaya was "adopted as daughter" by a woman of Nuzi, Tulpunnaya, known through numerous documents. The girl ran away but was forced back by a law-suit which her mistress had started against her.

Another document shows that Kisaya had a firm character and a will of her own. Her mistress had chosen for her as husband a man called Mannuya; Kisaya fought against it and insisted on being married to a certain Arteya, whom she obviously loved. Her steadfastness was successful: "Her word was made binding and Kisaya given to Arteya as his wife." The contract was sealed in the presence of seven witnesses. There is, however, a further contract which shows the fate of this slave in a few words, but all the more movingly. She declares: "My son Inziteshup, whom I have borne to Arteya, I have now given to Tulpunnaya." And to seal this transaction, Tulpunnaya cut off the seam of Kisaya's garment as a symbol for the incontestability of the contract. The document was drawn up at Nuzi approximately in the year 1450 B.C., in the presence of fourteen witnesses and is sealed with seven seals. (91, Nos. 30–33)

Of the documents from Nuzi some more are to be mentioned, because they are of interest for the legal status of a female slave, a certain Chanate. (91, Nos. 42–44) Chanate, too, was a slave of Tulpunnaya; she had evidently become wealthier and now tried to increase her fortune by imitating her mistress. She "adopted" a girl as "daughter" but shared her mistress' fate: the girl fled. The intervention of the court of law had the desired effect; the adopted daughter had to return and was married to a slave. That is what the facts say about the fate of this other "adopted daughter," but they disclose also something else of interest with regard to the legal position of a female slave in Nuzi: firstly, she could conclude legal transactions, for example an adoption; secondly, she could be a partner to a law-suit independently and without her mistress; and thirdly, being a well-to-do slave, she could herself keep slaves and deal with them like any free woman.

Several more instances are known from Nuzi, where slaves could play an important role in public life, when they had attained to a measure of prosperity. It has been reported that the female slave of a palace adopted a free man and made him heir to her possessions, including her slaves. (81, p. 72)

From other parts of the East and of other periods as well, some sources point to the chances offered sometimes to female slaves: in the New-Sumerian period (approx. 2000 B.C.), they could themselves act repeatedly in law-suits or could, if they possessed the means, buy their freedom. (21, p. 87)

In Ugarit many female slaves seem to have owned movable and immovable goods; they were given donations and freedom. This, however, is the rule only when they married a free man. (49)

It is known that a slave could work her way up by marriage or by liaisons, she even might become queen (the Parthian Queen Musa had been a slave) (Ill. 87). But these "dreamlike successes" tell little about the social life of the large mass of slaves. It has to be stressed again and again that only under particularly favourable conditions

22

were they able to gain any influence on their fate or to secure freedom. According to the general principle they were objects which by law could be sold, pawned, bequeathed, etc. The instances which became known of individual slaves in Nuzi, Ugarit, the Hittite empire and of the Neo-Babylonian period who conducted their own legal business and became affluent because of favourable conditions, are, it must be understood, exceptions. As we have seen, the laws contain, however, some provisions which secured for the slave, especially if she was a mother, a certain legal protection. Moreover, many rulers, usually at the beginning of their reign, made a promise to improve the position of the needy, the widows and the orphans, as well as that of the female and male slaves; the "reform-texts" of Urukagina have already been mentioned. A Hittite order of the king to his officials (approximately 13th century B.C.) to deal justly, and without accepting bribes, in legal affairs, also had a programme like this in view. "When the slave of a man, or the female slave of a man or a single woman is involved in a law-suit, decide it for her to her satisfaction" (97, p.48)—yet verbose declarations of this kind did nothing or little to remedy the abuses.

A few paragraphs and the above decrees cannot delude us from overlooking the fact that female slaves were personally not free and that their treatment and social position was often unworthy of human beings. Much of interest is to be found particularly in letters, but unfortunately also much that is unpleasant: reports of brutal force, beatings, chains. A certain Awīl-Adad wrote in a letter from ancient Babylon:

"I got hold of Sha-lā-ummi and mastered her by force. She cried, 'I am the slave of Bēlshunu, my mistress has given me to him.' I have beaten her and now have gone. Now I let her be taken to you. Put her in chains of five *minae* and lock her up. She still wants to come here, she will try to escape you. The chain ought to prevent this ..." (63, No.27)

The chief reason for such practices was the economic benefit that was to be gained. It is superfluous to emphasize that efficient business men and women specialized in the slave trade as it was remunerative, if one knew how to tackle "the job." One could for example "freshen-up" lean and inconspicuous looking female slaves in such a way that one could sell them at a profit; a letter speaks about this:

"We bought two female slaves at the price of one-third of a *mina* and three *shekel* silver. Shuma-ilum had not bought them because they were meagre. I have seen to it that they now look blooming and shall sell them. Do not ever look at the trifling amount of silver and do not buy anyone with a blemish; as long as a male or female slave is looking pale do not have anything to do with them." (63, No.139)

The letters often deal with the flight of female slaves and the endeavours of the masters or their agents to get hold of them again. From an account by King Abi-eshukh we gather that once all the servants of a certain Lamassanī had fled and that she had brought them back with the help of a man on horseback and one other official. (25, No.71) (Lamassanī was a nadītum from Sippar.)

Endeavours at escape by slaves from temples or palaces were comparatively frequent. The solidarity prevailing among these suppressed people is shown among others by a report from the Mari archive. The cook who had to bring fish to the palace, helped several persons to escape—among them a female slave—and was then himself wanted by the furious ruler, probably for punishment. (99)

There are several reports about organized revolts of slaves, which, however, brought about no fundamental change.

MATRIMONY AND FAMILY LIFE

In the previous chapter we discussed the position of woman in matrimony mainly from the point of view of the different esteem accorded to husband and wife. Now we shall turn to another aspect of matrimony and family life, which on the whole is more pleasant. We shall make use of those sources which report on woman as bride, as loving wife and mother. Much of what concerns love, matrimony and maternity has not been changed in the course of the centuries. But contrary to today, matrimony was chiefly a matter of utility and common sense, as the family of the Ancient East formed a kind of "emergency community," a union with the special aim of keeping its place in the surrounding world and to survive times of need under the patriarchal leadership of the *pater-familias*. A modern scholar described it pertinently as forming for the individual members of the family a "substitute for the then non-existent insurances against illness, disability or old age." (18) The family's existence was all the safer, the larger the number of its workers who were growing up; as a rule its economic basis therewith also widened. This instinct of self-preservation, aiming at the maximum of stability, even led to a kind of "family planning," with regard to the number of children and the choice of the right matrimonial partner. As to children, the aim was: the more the better and as many sons as possible. As to the matrimonial partner, it seems that the choice was not made according to sentiment, but to what was deemed useful and suitable for the welfare of the family. As a rule the choice was not left to the young people themselves, who might have been blinded by love, but was thought the duty of the father, and, after his death, of the mother or the elder brothers respectively, who then prepared the marriage carefully and with the greatest possible circumspection. This "choice" was sometimes made very early on, when the future matrimonial partners were still at a very youthful age; the "brides" seem not at all rarely to have been infants. In a Sumerian proverb a young man refuses to accept a three-year-old bride. (33, No. 2.81)

When the matrimonial arrangements were completed by the parents, the couple was already considered as being definitely committed and any renunciation was accompanied by financial loss. The law provided suitable fines for such cases and we may assume that this had been proved necessary. A frequent reason for the withdrawal from the contract seems to have been that the

Woman giving birth, making milk pour out of her breasts, mistress of animals

fiancé looked at another woman and said to his prospective father-in-law: "I shall not take your daughter" (CH paragraph 159). As a punishment he had to renounce all payments made so far to the bride's parents, the "bride's money" and the "engagement presents." In the opposite case the bride's father had to give to the rejected bridegroom twice the value of what he had received.

But assuming that such complications did not occur and that the engagement remained valid, the bride's father did well to watch carefully over his daughter, so that she might be handed over to the fiancé on the wedding day undefiled and as a virgin. Great importance was attached to the virginity of the young girl, in particular in the case of a "bargain marriage." Had a girl been raped, the man responsible for it had to marry her or to pay to the father the threefold price; had she already been engaged to be married, the death sentence awaited the criminal. According to a more recent Sumerian document (approximately 2000 B.C.) a young husband repudiated his wife, because she had not come to him as a virgin. (21, No. 205)

Before entering ceremoniously the bridal bed, tradition demanded that several formalities had to be observed. It was the custom for the bridegroom or his parents to pay a so-called "bride's money" *(tirchatum)* to the parents of the bride. This is the "bride's money" mentioned above together with the "engagement gift" *(biblum)*. The nature of the *tirchatum*, however, has not yet been unambiguously explained: it is taken to have been originally the purchase price for daughters bought from the parents. This was a far-spread custom in the Ancient East; thus the ancient Israelite laws stipulated that the father of the girl ought to be given "money according to the dowry of virgins" (Ex. 22, 15 seq.). This bride's money was always carried to the bride's house and there accepted ceremoniously by the parents. This and the pouring of oil over the bride's head was considered the sealing of the "marriage negotiations" and made everything binding for both partners.

Of decisive importance for the recognition of the marriage, with all legal consequences, seems to have been the contract: "When a man has taken a wife without a written commitment, then the woman is not a married woman" (CH paragraph 128, similar CE paragraphs 27, 28). Owing to the importance of this document, its drawing up took place in a greatly dignified and probably exciting ceremony; an official scribe wrote the text on a clay tablet in the presence of several witnesses. The bride, however, was only the "object" of these contracts, she took no active part nor spoke for herself; she was "given" by her parents, "taken" by her fiancé. But it may be assumed that not all brides accepted these customs uncritically; in a proverb a young girl complains about the bargaining and haggling between son-in-law and father-in-law over bride and bride's money. (33, No. 1. 169, 1) Yet she passed, as was the general custom of the Ancient East, from the domination of her father into that of her husband, which in ancient Babylonian times was made definite by a wording like this:

> "Ishtar-ummi, daughter of B. and of L., has accepted from B., her father, and from L., her mother, respectively Warad-Sin, the son of I., as her matrimonial partner. Her *tirchatum*, $^2/_3$ *mina* of silver, has been handed over by Warad-Sin to L. and B."
>
> (54, IV, No. 776)

By contrast, the young future husband often "spoke-up" when taking part in the negotiations, although one may assume that the father had previously assured the son of his consent to the marriage, as without the parents' agreement, it could be declared invalid. In a Neo-Babylonian marriage contract—composed in the then usual dialogue form—the bridegroom says to the bride's father:

> "Nabū-achu-iddina, son of Ap, spoke to Dalileshshu, son of Ar: 'Give me your virgin daughter Banāt-Esagila, to be my wife.' Dalileshshu granted this request and gave him his virgin daughter to be his wife ... Should Banāt-Esagila be found with another man, she is to be killed with an iron dagger. They swear by Nabū and Marduk, their gods, and by Nebuchadnezzar, the King, their lord, that this contract is not to be altered." (75, p. 7)

Fortunately, there are many more contracts extant, through which we can learn more details concerning matrimony in the Ancient East, for example that the daughter received a dowry from her parents, with which, however, her claim to inheritance was regarded as paid off. Jewellery "for the front of her neck," arm- and finger rings, precious stones, movable property, slaves, even whole families of slaves, landed property, in fact any real estate, could be given as dowry. According to the wealth of her parents, many a young bride represented a good match for her husband, and rich dowries no doubt facilitated the conclusion of many marriages. Together the married couple could use or increase what had been given as dowry; after the wife's death the dowry went to the children. In case of childlessness, the wife's parents claimed it to be returned to them, but the *tirchatum* paid by the bridegroom could be deducted therefrom. This, at least, is what the law was (CH paragraphs 162–164); and it clearly indicates that marriage, especially where money was concerned, was a transaction of economic importance. Documents from the law-courts confirm that there were frequent litigations about matters of inheritance or maintenance.

Having reported on these prerequisites for the marriage, we now can proceed to the description of the wedding festivities. As a rule the wedding took place in the house of the bride's father and was lavishly celebrated, the gay festivities lasting for days, if the economic situation allowed it. A quite unique text from Old-Babylon tells us about the wedding customs, and also shows that a wedding, suitable to the position of the bride's family, was bound to be very costly. (34) All expenditure for the wedding has been carefully noted in these accounts, and to their accuracy we owe a considerable amount of interesting information. We note that the family of the bride lived in the South-Mesopotamian town of Ur, but that the young husband came from the town of Larsa, at a distance of about 50 km. The first item in the long list of expenditure for which the bride's father was responsible, was the gift to the bridegroom; it consisted of a sum of money, a silver ring, one complete garment, coat and hat. Next follows the expenditure for gifts to the gods, as one was anxious to make sure of their benevolent agreement to the wedding. For safety's sake, sacrifices were made in both towns, in Ur and in Larsa. As soon as the guests arrived, large quantities of supplies were brought in, meal, beer of different kinds, cakes, lard, sheep to be slaughtered, sesame oil, fine oil for ointment, etc. The bridegroom's mother (who probably took the place of the defunct father) and those who brought the "wedding gift" are especially mentioned as guests. This gift most likely was something "eatable," provided by friends and near relatives of the bridegroom under his instruction, as a sign of the new relationship created by the marriage; it was a very old custom, as already the *Gilgamesh-Epic* tells of a man who brought a "wonderful wedding cake" to the wedding (Tablet IV, 22).

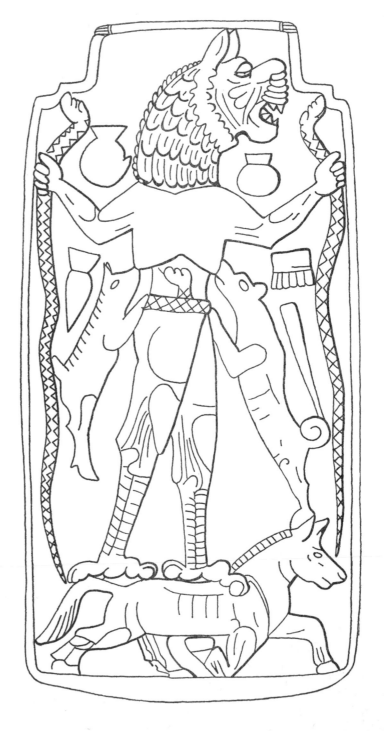

The father of the bride was not at all stingy in treating his guests; both at the time of their arrival and of their departure all his household was busy baking and slaughtering, and the "day of the bath" cost him an additional barrel of beer (probably to be used at the sacrifices). The bath on the wedding day was a ceremonious event, which in literature describing the wedding of gods is depicted with delight. Thus we read in a hymn for the so-called "Sacred Marriage" about the bath of the bride Inanna:

"My Lady bathes (her) golden loins in water,
for the loins of the king she bathes,
for the loins of Iddin-Dagan she bathes.
Pure Inanna rubs herself with soap-plant,
she sprinkles herself with aromatic cedar oil.
The king proudly goes to the pure loins,
to the loins of Inanna he goes proudly,
Ama'ushumgalanna goes to bed with her."

(34, p. 62)

On earth, too, the bride bathed herself with special care for her bridegroom; so as to be still more attractive when standing before him, she anointed herself with fragrant oil as preparation for entering the wedding bed. Aromatic oils and ointments were very popular in the Ancient East, the use of ointments being made necessary by the climate. Frequently ointments, together with garments and food, formed part of wages. For the care of the body plenty of fragrant oils were in use, for instance some gained from the cypress, the cedar or the myrtle, to which were frequently added other costly scents obtained from various kinds of resin, partly even imported from abroad. To make the eyes more expressive, the black eyebrows and the shape of the lids were enhanced by the use of antimony: coloured make-up, chiefly reddish and yellowish, helped to increase the charm and beauty of the woman's face. Gallipots for all kinds of make-up have been preserved in large numbers; they were probably much used by the brides at their weddings, in particular on the "bath day," which was one of the high points of the preparations for the festivities. This was the day on which, after the fragrant bath, the young couple was conducted to the festively decorated bed. It is noteworthy that the bridegroom remained for four months in his father-in-law's house and took his young wife only after that time to Larsa. The above mentioned ancient Babylonian text, which reports this,

also tells us that he was well cared for during this visit; for the day on which she left the expense for another sheep and for more bread and beer was recorded in the accounts.

Unfortunately, we learn nothing further about individual wedding ceremonies and customs or about their duration or chronological sequence. In this respect the sources are rather poor. Yet from various texts, documents, letters, etc. we at least gather that the "veiling" of the wife by her husband, in the presence of witnesses, symbolized the fact that she now was a married woman (MAss paragraph 42). "Headgear" too (63, No. 30; 70, p. 98), a "bonnet" (21, No. 26) and a "bridal crown" (70, p. 81), are mentioned and seem to have played a role of certain importance. In principle the covering of the head—be it with a veil, a bonnet or something else—was significant and testified that the marriage had taken place; the removing of the "garment pin" or the "virgin's garment pin" is also mentioned sometimes. (70, p. 104) Moreover, there are certain objects which symbolize the dignity of the married woman, as for instance the mirror or the spindle (Ill. 49, 56, 59, 62), or the young wife's own seal, with which she sealed deeds, letters and other documents. This was to show her respected position as the mistress of the house and of her personality as such. The concubine was not allowed to break that seal, as is stipulated in the marriage contract reprinted on page 16 of this book.

The young bride was now a married woman. If sympathy and love united the couple and they were soon blessed with children, this certainly led to harmonious and happy matrimony, which the artists of the Ancient East have frequently depicted as the loving unity of man and wife. Calmly standing side by side, hand in hand, or one arm around the other's shoulders, they symbolize the simple and honest union for life; its ethos and moral standing call for the greatest respect (Ill. 8, 28, 59). Although the keeping of concubines and slaves seems to contradict this, as does also the patriarchal organization of matrimony, which withholds from the wife the right to contradict her husband; yet this subordination of the wife does not necessarily mean lack of love and sympathy; the texts which have come down to us confirm this. Husband and wife shared life with each other, and their solidarity has been documented in many still extant private letters which they wrote to each other when they were separated. There is no lack of testimonials to the respect felt by the husband for his wife, his love of the children and his appreciation of family life. Many husbands made considerable donations to their wives (frequently of real estate), so as to safeguard her livelihood in case of his premature death. Clauses were introduced into the contract to protect her against objections by relatives and children. (21, p. 128 seq.) Instances of the most loving relationship between husband and wife have particularly been found in Susa. (45, p. 90 seq.; 50)

Thus, the donation made by the husband to his wife was once indicated by him in the following way: "... Because she has cared for him and worked for him, he has given and donated to her" (16th century B.C.). Many proverbs, the so-called "Wisdom Literature" etc., extol the merit of the woman as wife and mother, and highly appreciate the family as the safeguard of security (though there are also, of course, detracting remarks, as can always be found in literature). In one proverb the wife is called the "refuge" of the husband, the son "his future" and the daughter his "salvation." A "toast" enumerates what a man needs and adds the following good wishes for him:

"May Inanna cause a hot-limbed wife to lie down for
May she bestow upon you broadarmed sons.   [you.
May she seek out for you a place of happiness."

(33, No. 1.147.1)

The family, an able and efficient "hot-limbed" wife who bears him good sons and daughters, were the aim that was worth aspiring to more than any other for a man.

Due to this principle, it is not surprising that anything that tended to make a woman barren was forbidden. Abortion was thought to be one of the most outrageous crimes. Women guilty of it were punished cruelly: according to law they were impaled and denied internment (MAss paragraph 53).

The sources sometimes give hints of endeavours to prevent pregnancy. One relied—although in vain—on the magic of certain stones to exclude the natural consequences of coition. In particular priestesses, who according to law were to be childless, were anxious to prevent conception. It was said that because of this they allowed only an unnatural intercourse. (7) According to legends the gods placed the sexual taboo on some groups of priestesses so as to prevent too great an increase of the population. (92, p. 141)

In an oriental family of ancient times it certainly was a day of rejoicing when a child, preferably a son, was born. Children meant the continuation of the family, security for the future and old age, workers, and last but not least, joy and happiness. Quite often other children were adopted to add to the number of one's own. The birth of the first child was of course expected with the greatest excitement. Pregnancy and birth, however, were threatened by various dangers, for which one thought malign demons to be responsible, especially the female demon Lamashtum. She was greatly feared by young mothers, as she furtively grabbed the new-born and killed them, trying at the same time to kill also the young mothers with puerperal fever or similar means. Her mere appearance was terrifying, because

"Enlil had given her the face of a bitch;
She has miserable hands, over-long fingers,
Over-long finger nails; her elbows are dirty.
She enters the house by the outer door,
sneaks in at the pole-piece of the door,
When she has sneaked in at the pole-piece,
she kills the little one,
She grips him seven times at his belly ..."   (102)

Terrified, one tried to prevent the coming of the demon by incantations and magical ceremonies; amulets with her image were to influence her favourably and thereby to avert the danger from mother and child. One implored especially the goddesses who were supposed to be particularly well disposed towards pregnant women and those giving birth, for instance Nintu, Nininsina, Ninchursag (Ill. 13 a, 31, 50). Powers were ascribed to them "to let the foetus develop in the right way, so that the child of man, nursed on his lap, cries out loud." (94, p. 295)

On the day of the birth well-meaning relatives and neigbours were sure to be present, but it was the midwife who started to act, "she who knows the inside." (103) She helped the young mother not only with her practical knowledge, but also with all kinds of enchantment and magical arrangements, as the bad forces had to be staved off and the helping gods simultaneously encouraged and called forth in these crucial hours. Help at promoting the birth was expected especially from conjuring the mythical cow Gi-Sin, the "servant of Sin," who, having copulated with the moon god, had been unable to give birth. When her hour had come, Sin ordered two heavenly

deities to bring "the water of the birth-pangs" and oil. When he had touched her eyebrows with the oil and sprinkled her with the water, she was happily able to give birth. The formula which was hoped to give magic help to the mother runs: "As Gi-Sin, the servant of Sin, happily gave birth, thus may also this young wife be delivered from her pains." These pains made her appear a picture of wretchedness:

"Like a warrior in the fray, she is cast down in her
Her eyes are diminished, she cannot see, [blood.
her lips are covered,
. . . her eyes are dim,
. . . her ears cannot hear.
Her breast is not . . ., her locks are scattered,
she wears no veil and has no shame.
Be present and . . ., merciful Marduk."   (69, p. 32)

In the ancient oriental *Etana legend* the suffering of a mother in confinement forms the basis for the story of a "cosmic flight" on the wings of an eagle: When his wife was in confinement, Etana wanted to fetch a birth-furthering herb from heaven, mounted an eagle and flew ever higher and higher—while the view of the earth seen perspectively is described. Eventually he crashed down with the eagle and could not get the herb. Therefore mothers, not even excepting goddesses, have still to suffer pains. A Sumerian text from Nippur says: Even Ereshkigal, the goddess of the nether world, "lies down ill" when in childbed, ". . . she has put the hair of her head together like a leek, she screams: Woe to my inside." (59, p. 9 seq.)

Even when the young mother, crouching or seated on a delivery chair (Ill. 1), has been lucky to bring her child into the world, and forgets all past misery, the new-born infant had to be inspected carefully to see whether its condition did not portend disaster. One tried to find out about the future fate of the child with the help of omens, later even of horoscopes. It sometimes happened that a child was exposed, partly because of superstition, partly because of want. If they did not die, such children generally ended in slavery. Frequently priestesses, on whom virginity or childlessness was prescribed, were accused of exposing their children. According to legend the great Sargon of Akkad was a child exposed by a high-priestess; he was then cared for by a gardener; and according to the Old Testament the Pharaoh's daughter recovered the infant Moses in a basket of rushes from the water (Ill. 92). But in normal economic and family situations the exposure of children was probably rare.

After the birth the midwife lifted up the child to present it to the father, as described by a Hittite fairy tale: "She lifted up the child and dandled it on Appu's knees. Appu began to be glad of the child, started to fondle it and gave it the sweet name of 'Bös' . . ." (27)

As a rule it seems to have been the father who gave the child the name. The name could express a wish—"May he live," "Be mother's pet" (or "Father's pet")—or it might recommend the child to the particular favour of a god ("The sun god is my guardian god"). Qualities of the child also appear as names, as "Small" or "Bald," and sometimes an event characteristic of the child's birth is used as its name: "She has born a strong one" or "He jumped up to the roof," a name pointing to the joy of the father, which could hardly have been shown in a more charming way.

The hope of the father centred mainly around a son; he, possibly with younger brothers, would inherit, and after the parents' death perform the required death ceremonies, so as to save the parents from restless roaming about in the realm of the dead. There are, however, also many testimonials to show that many an unwanted daughter was later-on much loved by her parents and had not to accept a place inferior to that of her brothers. Fathers frequently seem to have been especially fond of their daughters: the Elamite King Shilhak-Inshushinak (1150–1120 B.C.) had a charming idea to give pleasure to his youngest daughter, Bar-Uli. He handed her a large bead of blue chalcedony and had a picture incised in it showing that very moment as well as the words: "For my beloved daughter Bar-Uli." The little lady is seen standing before him accepting the precious gift from the father, who already had seven other children, for none of whom we know of so loving an inscription as for this evidently best beloved child (Ill. 42).

Other fathers, too, some of them royal ones, have left to us in various manners, be it on stelae or stones or in simple letters, proofs of their fatherly love for their daughters (Ill. 51). Frequently, they made personal donations to them; this is confirmed by numerous instances mainly from Susa, where wives and daughters enjoyed a specially favourable position. (50)

Documents from Nuzi report that daughters were sometimes given by the father the right to exercise paternal authority with regard to younger brothers: "She may act as if she were I." If the brothers missed showing the respect due to her, she could make them slaves, even disinherit them. (105)

While daughters often received proofs of love and respect from their fathers, the mothers loved still more not only their sons but also their daughters and cared for them as much as possible. In their earliest years the children were usually left in the care of the mother. She suckled them herself or engaged, if she was sufficiently well off, a wet nurse by contract. According to these contracts from old Babylon, the wet nurse remained in charge of the child (suckled it?) for two to three years; her wage consisted of garments, oil for ointment and of her food. (54, III, Nos. 32–34)

The mother was the stable centre for the children in the family, looking after their needs, and preparing food for them. In cuneiform tablets from approximately 2000 B.C. we can read that she supplied the boys going to school with "small breads" (58, p. 24), and that she gave them little gifts when they were old enough to study cuneiform writing. The rather amusing begging-letter written by a student with the nickname "Monkey" to his mother is probably one of the oldest of this kind—it dates from the year 2000 B.C. Like so many later ones, it told her that the son had no money and that he hoped the mother would send him some by a fast messenger:

"To Ludiludi, my mother, say:

thus says 'Monkey':

'Ur is the town of the joy of Nanna,

Eridu is the town of Enki's luxury;

I, however, sit behind the door of the house of the great singers

and eat garbage.

May I not die of it!

Bread, I never taste, never taste an intoxicating drink!

Send me a fast messenger.

Urgent!'" (57)

Besides this the letter from another young "student," Iddin-Sin, seems quite modern, too. He bitterly complains to his mother Zinu that the garments which she let him have, from year to year are of poorer quality. While Adadiddinam, "whose father is only an employee of my father, has received two new sets of garments, you are irritated about a single one for me. And this, though you are my real mother, while his mother has only adopted him, but she loves him, and you, you do not love me." (89, No. 16, p. 84).

This shows that the mothers in Antiquity met with various problems with their children, especially if, according to the ancient oriental ideal family, they had to bring up a large number of sons. This has often been shown rather picturesquely by proverbs. Thus it has been said that a mother with eight growing up sons—evidently afraid of the ninth—entered her husband's

Mother suckling child

bed only "passively" although she could quite well bear more sons. And another proverb stresses the difficulty of educating sons, as it was more difficult to "silence" them than daughters. (33, No. 2, 141.1; 1.185.1)

Important decisions about education were the responsibility of the father. He also informed the sons about intimate questions, told them about hierodules and prostitutes and gave them his advice.

We, however, are more interested in the education of daughters. While the sons of noble houses (unfortunately, the sources refer almost only to these) were given early on a suitable education preparing them for their future profession—learning to write and read the difficult cuneiform script was one of the main items—the girls were chiefly occupied in the house, with the aim of marrying them off as good as possible; the best thing one could wish the father of the family was, "may all your daughters marry." (60, p. 214)

The girls were taught certainly all they had to know for matrimonial life. Apart from housework they learned all kinds of female handicrafts, and were equally well experienced in music, dance and singing (Ill. 51). Many women and young girls were also taught to write, which was done mostly in the temple or convent service or at court. Nor does there seem to have been any lack of play, fun or flirtation for young girls with this background. The fragment of a myth which has only recently been republished, describes the gay and happy day of the young goddess Inanna, which probably resembled that of many a young girl of the Ancient East. Inanna who "spent all the day playing and singing songs until nightfall, met in the market the young man who adored her, who embraced her impetuously and askd her to make love; she refused because she could think of no excuse to tell her mother, but she was soon told what to say:

"My girl friend played with me in the market,
 playing with hand-drums and drumsticks she ran
 about with me,
—her songs are pleasant, she sang for me.
With her I spent all the time!"   (115)

It seems that at that time, the young girls enjoyed themselves as much as today, though for the music they made they had to use drums worked with their own hands and not transistor radios as today. Rulers frequently mention that children sing happily, so as to demonstrate how good and blissful their rule is. (48, p. 321)

Yet everyday life was not happy and without worries for all children and young people, as is shown by the documents concerning the sale of children and youths. They were given away for money by their parents if the latter got into economic difficulties, of which there are many reports particularly from the Neo-Sumerian and the Larsa periods. Testimonies of such sad existences have, however, come down to us also from Nuzi and Assyria, and sales of children are repeatedly being reported from the Neo-Babylonian period. (81, p. 5 seq.; 21, p. 85; 55, No. 39)

As a rule it was the daughters who were sold, sons more seldom; often it happened in their youth, even their childhood. Once grown up, many of them tried to challenge their slavedom with legal proceedings, as is shown by documents of the Neo-Sumerian courts of law. The fathers and mothers, too, made attempts of this kind, but nearly always without any success, so that those who had been sold were left in the power of the buyer or his heirs. (21, No. 35, 37, 46, 47, 50, 54)

Compared, however, with other documents, it has to be stated that those about the sale of children by their parents were not too frequent. Where the sales happened in larger numbers, they seem to indicate a general social regression; the people of the ancient Orient with their pronounced family pride, certainly made use of this desperate means only in dire necessity. An oriental proverb says: "A poor man does not strike his son a single blow; he treasures him forever." (33, No. 2.23) Children were all the wealth of the simple man, they were his "treasure," though also an "asset" which he could use for payments if he could find no other way out, as, according to another proverb, the poor man lives "off what is paid for his children." (68, p. 248)

Yet one must not think that the sale of children points to a disrupted and loveless relationship between parents and children. We must try to understand them as a consequence of the general conditions prevailing at that time. For those economically weak the sale of members of the family or of themselves was often the only means of survival.

In this chapter only the "normal" ancient oriental marriage has been discussed, the "monogamous" marriage of one man married to one woman. Yet, as is well known, the wife had under certain conditions to agree to her husband taking a concubine, who, however, had to recognize her authority as "mistress" and was not allowed to put herself on a par with her. Marriages remained not always as "normal" and harmonious as has been described in this chapter. But as marriages where concubines were included have already been discussed in detail, this chapter may now be closed and the story proceed to a new one.

But before doing so, one ought to summarize by stating that, as many instances show, the married woman in the Ancient East did not always find it easy to live with her husband, the family or the children. As far, however, as the prevailing conditions allowed, she always safeguarded her rights and did her duty in society as well as in the family as wife and mother.

"SACRED MARRIAGE" AND "LIFTING UP OF THE HEART"

Man in the Ancient East gave himself up ardently and passionately to the joys of life. He loved love and lust and used a remarkable inventiveness to enjoy life by day and night with all his senses. One could collect quite a number of maxims stating that it is delightful and worth aspiring after, to taste all the sweetness of existence without any reservation. This principle is, however, often based on the knowledge that, on the whole, life is difficult and toilsome, a continuous up and down. In an earlier, paradisical, unfortunately long past era, everybody had been happy; there had been no struggle for existence, no war, no destruction, no tax-collector, but well-being and joy everywhere. Now man ought to give himself up twice as eagerly to the good hours of life, as calamities and misfortunes may soon overcome him. (58)

There are frequent hints that the gods, too, are not reliable. According to the *Epic of Gilgamesh*, they assigned to themselves "life," but to mankind "death." Considering the transience and illusiveness of life and fortune, the "hero of Uruk" is advised:

"... Fill, oh Gilgamesh, your belly,
Enjoy yourself day and night,
Arrange daily a festivity for yourself,
With dance and play by day and night.
Let your garments be brilliantly clean,
Wash your head and bathe in water,
Look at the child who takes your hand!
And may your wife rejoice in your arms,
For all this forms man's happiness."

(96, tablet No. 10, 6–14)

Here the man of the Ancient East has put together what made life worth living for him: beside a comfortable existence without daily worries, chiefly a quiver full of children and the enjoyment of love. And he always gladly paid the tribute due to love.

The previous chapters have already shown that it was mainly the man, at whose disposal were various means to pursue sensual pleasures. The principal wife, concubines and pretty female slaves could secure for their lord and master many happy hours. Besides, public prostitutes offered their charms everywhere in the streets; and finally there were the slaves of the temple who acted as sacred prostitutes in the service of the goddess. It would be wrong to judge this naively-unhampered enjoyment of the senses by modern standards. In the areas under the influence of Christian religion sex has almost been

Couple of the "Sacred Marriage" (?)

reckoned among the sins, but in the old oriental religions it has a natural place. Coition was elevated to a sanctified act in worship, and even prostitution with its originally sacred concept was not objectionable or immoral, except for later development. We can, therefore, not do justice to the woman of the Ancient East if we exclude from the description of her life the mention of the role played by sex, which accounted for so much of it.

A religion with anthropomorphic gods, acting like men—also with regard to love and sensual pleasures—naturally reserved for sex in the family and in public life a space so wide we can nowadays hardly visualize.

Owing to this purely instinctive attitude, the man of the Ancient East spoke of love and begetting quite without any scruples or moral hesitation. Because of this candour, many texts and pictorial representations are still kept unpublished in the depots of museums, and there is still a total lack of any comprehensive treatment of the subject as a whole, as scholars have so far always approached it with great reserve. The modern reader is therefore usually offered only a selection, which has passed the filter of what is "presentable." Anyway, the sources have not yet been completely exhausted. Nevertheless, the material obtainable shows well enough the range of the relevant facts in cult as well as in everyday life. Representations of couples of lovers united in a close embrace date back at least to the 9th millennium B.C. They probably were to symbolize and enhance, through some magic power fertility, propagation and sexual strength. Written testimonials referring to sexual love follow, however, only some millennia later. Yet one can state fairly safely that one of the oldest love songs of world literature has been written in the Ancient East, in Sumer. The bridegroom is tenderly praised by this song:

"Bridegroom, dear to my heart,
goodly is your beauty, honeysweet,
Lion, dear to my heart,
goodly is your beauty, honeysweet.
You have captivated me, let me stand tremblingly before you,
Bridegroom, I would be taken by you to the
Bridegroom, let me caress you,   [bedchamber.
my precious caress is more savory than honey,
in the bedchamber, honey-filled,
let me enjoy your goodly beauty.
You, because you love me,

give me pray of your caresses,
my lord god, my lord protector,
my Shu-Sin, who gladdens Enlil's heart,
give me pray of your caresses."

(57, p. 170, abbreviated)

The last lines disclose that this is not only a profane love song, which a girl sings to her lover. The speaker, and the King Shu-Sin to whom she speaks, are the chief actors in the so-called "Sacred Marriage," the important festival of love and fertility, which was celebrated in the Ancient East in connection with the New Year festivities with great pomp, with music and feasting. It was the wedding feast of a divine couple, of the youthful and beautiful love-and mother-goddess and of her divine lover, which was excuted ceremoniously by their earthly deputies: the king, the high-priest respectively, and the high-priestess. According to contemporary beliefs they furthered by this orgiastic ritual a new and strong fertility for man, animal and earth. The goddess ordained the king to "the fate of ruling" for a further year. Details of the ritual are not known; but the texts repeatedly refer to a preciously decorated bed, as it was suitable for a sacred ritual marriage, an indispensable piece of furniture. Further, there are frequent descriptions of the lovely divine bride taking a luxurious bath, making herself attractive with jewellery and fragrant oils, all this as preparation for the wedding festivities. These began with the recitation of love-songs referring to the sacred ceremonial and then progressed with music and an "intoxicating drink" to its zenith, the "marriage" of the chosen exalted couple. They probably ended with a general orgy of everyone participating in the festivities.

The origin of this ritual is to be seen in the popular Sumerian cult of Inanna-Dumuzi in which Inanna, goddess of love and fertility, was united with Dumuzi, a deified (legendary?) king of the town of Uruk. According to the legend Dumuzi, the lover of the goddess Inanna, descended every year in the hot and arid summer months to the nether world, and returned to earth again in spring. His "death" and return symbolized the death and re-awakening of nature, and by the auspicious and glorious union of the resurrected Dumuzi with the goddess of love at the beginning of the new year, man and earth gained—as was generally believed—new strength and new life through magic forces. The kings of the Third Dynasty of Ur and of the Isin Dynasty (for example Shu-Sin, Shulgi, Amarsu'en, Iddin-Dagan, Ishme-Dagan, and many others) acted, especially in the role of Dumuzi, as bridegroom in the Sacred Marriage. It should also be mentioned that the *Gilgamesh Epic*, too, speaks of the Sacred Marriage: in the second tablet (V, 28 seq.), we can read that the hero went to the "uncovered bed" of the goddess Ishcharat, to "unite himself with her at night."

Up to the 4th century B.C., this ceremony seems to have been rather wide-spread in the Ancient East, although it certainly was celebrated in different ways in individual areas and periods. We still have detailed descriptions of these New Year celebrations of the middle of the first millennium B.C. The great god Marduk "hurried to the wedding" with his divine Sarpanītu, and Nabū laid down on the "bed of the sweet night again and again to sweet sleep." (22)

Ashurbanipal, the famous Assyrian king (7th century B.C.), once donated a particularly valuable bed for the wedding of the gods: "As ceremonial bed I donated a bed of lasting wood, decorated with choice stones," he states in an inscription (Bauer, *Das Inschriftenwerk Assurbanipals II*, 1933, 31).

No doubt, the small terracotta beds with a nude couple resting on them in loving embrace (Ill. 27 a, b, c) are connected with the Sacred Marriage. These attractive "bed idols" stem from various periods and are preserved in a large number of varieties. Probably they were even worn as pendants from the neck, as recently revealed by a very interesting and so far unique statuette: a high-priestess, certainly the bride of the Sacred Marriage, wears as necklace a small precious bed on a chain. A couple of nude lovers is seen on it, in an embrace, the lofty couple of the *hieros gamos* (Ill. 26) (108)—an important pictorial testimonial for the celebration of this ritual in Early Dynastic times (mid-third millennium B.C.).

These wedding scenes have also been reproduced in an "abbreviated" simplified form; instead of showing the couple in relief, the female symbol only was incised (a triangle or a rhombus) and everybody knew what this meant. All these representations of beds certainly served as symbols and magic of fertility.

It seems likely that many of the songs recited at the Sacred Marriage—or parts of them—were composed by the priestesses, who took part in the ritual, as often quite individual experiences and events are mentioned:

"Because I uttered the allari-song,
the lord gave me a gift, a
pendant of gold, a seal of lapislazuli ..."
(58, p. 252)

They also show true feelings, tenderness and poetic art:

"... the people will set up my fruitful bed
they will cover it with plants (the color of) durulapis
I will bring there my sweetheart,   [lazuli,
I will bring there Ama'ushumgalanna,
he will put his hand by my hand,
he will put his heart by my heart.
His putting of hand to hand—its sleep is so refreshing
his pressing of heart to heart, its pleasure is so sweet."
(61, p. 496)

The brides never hesitate to give their "lovers" attractive descriptions of their enticing charms:

"My god, of the wine-maid, sweet is her drink,
like her drink sweet is her vulva, sweet is her drink.
Like her lips sweet is her vulva, sweet is her
drink ..."   (58, p. 252)

Some of the priestesses taking part in the Sacred Marriage as "brides" are known to us by name: the partners of the above mentioned King Shu-Sin were his "much loved priestess Abbabashti," of whom a magnificent piece of golden agate jewellery has been preserved, and the priestess Kubatum.

Encheduanna, en-priestess of the god Nanna and daughter (?) of Sargon of Akkad (approx. 2300 B.C.), was probably also a bride of the Sacred Marriage. She became famous through a fairly long poem of her own; her likeness has been preserved in a relief (Ill. 21).

As a rule the brides of the *hieros gamos* were priestesses of the highest rank. They were influential and important personalities, who, as representatives of the mighty and "great" gods, occupied correspondingly dominating positions. They were elected for their high office by a "liver omen," that is the examination of the liver of a sacrificed animal for its prophetic qualities; then they were given the special insignia of their dignity. Frequently they were members of the ruling family. They had a residence of their own where, possibly, the Sacred Marriage may have been celebrated. (92, p. 118 seq.) The activities of these high-priestesses, their personal participation in the venerable and important ceremony of the Sacred Marriage, must on no account be confused with what is usually designated as "temple prostitution." This prostitution, practised as part of the cult by lower-grade priestesses, the hierodules, was, like the Sacred Marriage, based on the "mystic veneration of the process of begetting as a divine act" (48, p. 476), but it deteriorated in the course of the centuries. What originally had been the sanctified ritual of fertility, was gradually made plain prostitution, and "business." In particular during the great temple festivities, strangers were attracted by the practices of the hierodules and the chests of the temple were filled with plentiful takings. Herodotus, in his *History*, recorded his observations of the practices in Babylonian temples, as well as any information received about them. This has considerably contributed to the general assumption that shamelessness and moral decline were excessive and widespread in the Ancient East. As most reprehensible, he points to the fact that, before marrying, all girls had, in honour of the goddess of love, to give up in her grove their virginity to any stranger from the street. (I, 199) This custom can be interpreted as a kind of *ius primae noctis* where the "stranger" symbolizes the "god". There are few proofs of this privilege in the Ancient East, but according to the *Epic*, Gilgamesh himself, king and hero of Uruk, exercised this right, as for him "the bed was opened among all his people." (96, tablet 2, IV, 18 seq.)

Herodotus' report certainly ought to be read with some reservation. On no account should it be accepted as applying to the temples of all goddesses of love in the ancient Orient. Yet the so-called sacred or temple prostitution no doubt formed part of fertility cults of the Ancient East. In some towns there seem to have been particularly numerous hierodules of various kinds. Uruk, for example, was called already in the middle of the 2nd millennium "the town of strumpets, prostitutes and harlots," and in the *Gilgamesh Epic* it is praised as the place where there are "prostitutes of lovely appearance and enriched by passion, and promising untold delight" (tablet 1, V, 10 seq.). About the range of the activities of the individual hierodules we unfortunately can say only very little. There were priestesses of different ranks and duties, among them groups quite clearly marked for sexual practices, dedicated to the temple prostitution in honour of the goddess. To these belonged in the Old-Babylonian period mainly the qadishtum, the ishtaritum and the kulmashitum; but, as said above, about them, as about other classes of hierodules from the various epochs and areas, far too little is known. (92) The girls

36

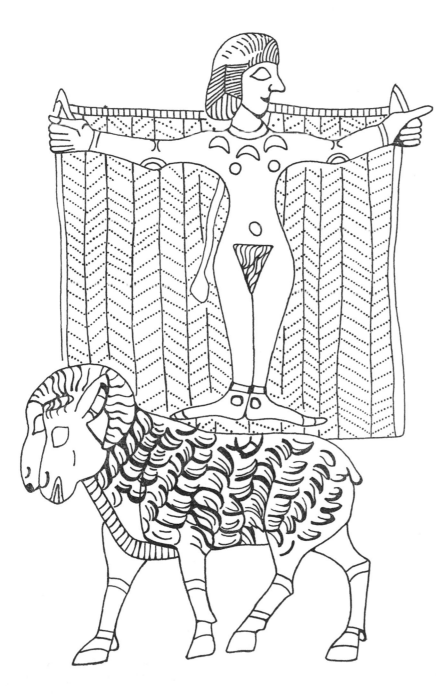

Nude goddess, standing on a ram

perfomed their duties probably in the main inside the precinct of the temple, in the "house with the place for love;" but their presence "in the street" and in the "shade of the wall" is also mentioned. A Hittite document tells us that they were subordinated to a female "warden" (ZA NF 19, 1959, 181).

n some of the temples of the Ancient Near East benches built like altars have been excavated, which were used by the hierodules. Moreover, numerous representations have been found, showing them performing their duties. These and similar scenes were probably used for amulets providing magic for fertility or love, etc. (Ill. 76a, b, 77). Small sculptures of the male or female genitals also seem to have been used as amulets, hung on a thread around the neck.

Generally the services which the hierodules performed for their deity were not thought dishonourable; the goddesses themselves—Inanna, Nininsina, Ninlil, Nintu, Ishtar, Anat and many others—were designated by the epithet "hierodule" or "heavenly hierodule" who "proudly fulfilled their duties as hierodules." There are many images showing this aspect of the goddess of love: with alluring limbs and clothing gathered up at the side or as "nude goddess" with unmistakeable sex appeal, as the great divine hierodule and seducer (Ill. 39). Thus, too, she certainly was the model for her young priestesses on earth. Dumuzi, the mythical husband of the goddess Inanna, in particular sympathized with the practices of the hierodules and let them do their work "again and again in the market squares of Kulaba" (ZA NF 22, 1964, p. 110), and also arranged for himself to be entertained by prostitutes playing the flute. That couples copulated in the "streets" and "market places" is mentioned frequently and seems to have been thought neither unusual nor objectionable. (44, p. 77)

It is certainly worth noticing that the *Gilgamesh Epic*, the most admired and popular poem of Sumerian-Babylonian literature, reserved a special and quite outstanding role for one of the hierodules of the goddess of love. She was destined to turn the wild uncivilized Enkidu, a savage living among the beasts of the field, sharing their food and drinking water at their wateringplace, into a "man." Through her arts she was to make him forget the animals and his wild life as a barbarian, in a word to "civilize" him, so that he could become the friend and comrade in arms of the hero, Gilgamesh.

These are the relevant passages of the *Gilgamesh Epic:*

"... bring here a hierodule from the temple
That her arts may overpower this man.
When he takes the wild beasts to their watering-place,
She is to uncover herself, let him see her naked.
When he sees her, he will approach her,
And the wild beasts
Who grew up in the steppe, will flee him ...
Then the prostitute made her breasts bare,
And when he approached her
Was without shame,
She took off her garment, that he might possess her body,
She incited him to love.
She welcomed his eagerness,
And taught him the woman's art.
Six days and seven nights passed,
While Enkidu lay with her
Until he was satisfied by her charms.
The beasts of the steppe shrank back from him,
And Enkidu was frightened, his body was benumbed
His knees gave way as the wild animals fled from him,
He was grown weak, and it was no more as it had been,
But he now had wisdom; he understood.
'Well, get up now from the earth,
Which once had been the poor bed of the shepherd,'
He heard her words, accepted her advice,
The woman's advice suited him;
Then she took Enkidu's hand
And led him, as one leads a child,
To the place where the shepherds slept near their flocks.
He used to suck the milk of the wild beasts—
Now they placed their food before him.
He was uneasy, opened wide his eyes
And stared at it: Enkidu did not know
What bread was and how to eat it.
Nor had he learned to drink beer.
Then the prostitute opened her lips
And said to Enkidu: 'Eat now the bread
Oh Enkidu, as that forms part of life,
Drink also some of the beer, as is the custom of this country.'
So Enkidu ate of the bread to his heart's desire
And drank of the beer his seven beakers.
His heart became light, he was happy,
He became gay and his face radiated.

He rubbed with water his body covered with hair,
Then anointed his limbs with oil,
And thus came to look like a human being;
When finally he put on garments
Nothing distinguished him any more from a man."

(96, from tablets 1 and 2)

[See *The Epic of Gilgamesh, An English Version, with an Introduction by N. K. Sandars,* Penguin Classics, 1965.]

Thus the hierodule had turned the savage Enkidu into a "man," had taught him morals and manners. It would be an exaggeration to state that there was a close connection between all activities of the hierodules and education, yet there can be no doubt that the temples were the centres from which knowledge and culture spread. There were schools which taught the cuneiform script and other contemporary knowledge. The priestesses were specially trained for the duties the cult prescribed for them, that is in particular for dancing, singing and music and certain ceremonial performances. Whatever their special function was, they enjoyed a certain amount of education, "culture" and morals, although, according to modern concepts, this does not agree well with the idea of prostitution; but as said above, one must not apply modern standards. The social position of the hierodule as representative and servant of the respective fertility-or love-goddess was no doubt originally much respected. She could marry, if she found a suitor, and then take the dignified place of a legitimate wife. It seems that she was still regarded as a member of her paternal family, while she retained her post as hierodule, as a late Babylonian document speaks of a *nu-bar*, a temple hierodule, who was given in marriage, according to custom, by her brother, the head of the family (ZA NF 21, 1962, 91 seq.). The maintenance list of an Assyrian temple points to a kind of "employment" of the hierodules and their children, and to certain supplies given to them. (17) From time to time there are reports about children of hierodules showing that people liked to adopt them. But frequently they remained in the temple and were dedicated to the deity or given to her as a "gift."

In the course of time profane prostitution gained an ever larger domain; in streets and markets the hierodules met with the competition of public prostitutes. The increasing social differentiation, middle-classes gradually declining into lower and poorer ones, induced many women and young girls to take up prostitution as a means

38

of making a living. Fathers sold their daughters; the contracts of these sales were often camouflaged as "adoptions;" yet they clearly state: She "shall be made a prostitute, and from her earnings she shall provide for . . . her mother." (81, p. 21) Slaves were increasingly used for this trade, providing their owner with a source of income. It has been proved that the "Bank" of Murashu and Sons, a large firm dealing with every kind of business, rented out prostitutes to procuresses. This development influenced also the status of the hierodules, who were active for purposes of the cult, and their social level sank to that of the prostitutes. Assyrian laws of the middle period dealing with the veiling of women are an instance of this (MAss paragraph 40): they strictly forbid unmarried hierodules, prostitutes and female slaves on pain of severe punishment to veil themselves or to cover their head; this was the privilege of respectable Assyrian women. The hierodules, like the prostitutes, had evidently reached the lowest social level and were almost made the equals of slaves. Fathers warned their marriageable sons not to marry prostitutes:

"Do not marry a prostitute (charimtu), whose husbands
[are legion,
a temple harlot (ishtaritum) who is dedicated to a god,
a courtesan (kulmashitum) whose favours are many.
In your trouble she will not support you,
in your dispute she will be a mocker."   (68, p. 103)

For an honourable father it was the worst possible shame if his daughters were cursed to be dedicated to the goddess Ishtar (see inscription for the goddess, Ill. 54), and in the *Gilgamesh Epic* we find, on the one hand, the curse for a temple prostitute, on the other a *laudatio*, a hymn of praise for her, indicating the double nature of her position. (96, tablet 7, III and IV) This applies also to the goddess of love herself, whose art of loving is highly praised and extolled, but is also despised and reviled. She is again and again blamed for all the evil "caused by her lust." Although old men "shake their head" about the temple prostitute, the younger men "smite their thighs" when they see them, and the youths "loosen their belts." Many a young man was captured by the voluptuous charms of such a prostitute and disregarded all moral scruples, as was said of him by a Sumerian text: "He picked her up in the street and married her for love while she was a hierodule" (ZA NF 22, 1964, 124).

Numerous critical passages in texts of this kind make us realize that the hierodule who in the *Gilgamesh Epic* had taught the savage and licentious man morals and manners, had now herself been declared infamous. And the members of this profane prostitution, who even lacked the cult's sanctification of the hierodule, were of course still less respected by honourable and austere men or women. Calling anyone a "prostitute" was something monstrous and could call for an ordeal to convict either the calumniator or the accused; marriage could be broken up, as is shown by an Old-Babylonian text: "Why have you calumniated the daughter of a citizen, your equal, and called her a prostitute, so that her husband left her?" (67, p. 195)

The women of this profession seem frequently to have exercised their trade in public houses and inns. These were, anyway, thought to be the meeting places of all kinds of rabble, and were looked at with suspicion by the legislator. Probably they often deserved to be called "public houses" in the sense of brothels. Respectable priestesses like the entum or the nadiātum were forbidden on pain of death to enter a public house (CH paragraph 110). Possibly this is to show a purposeful discrimination between them and the profane prostitutes who lived there, and with whom those dedicated to the goddess were not allowed to entertain any connection. Houses of this kind were to be found everywhere. The decisions of the courts and similar documents make it clear that a rather low standard of morals prevailed there. Yet the legislator has not denied even the prostitutes his protection and certain social rights, especially when they had borne children to a married man (CH paragraphs 27, 30; MAss paragraph 52). Even if she was not well spoken of, the prostitute originally was not lacking freedom. It seems that it was only the laws of the mid-Assyrian period which, as already mentioned, made her into an enslaved person, and it is the Persian sources which treat her with the greatest contempt.

It is rather surprising and comforting to read that the prostitutes were, nevertheless, proud of their "profession." They boasted of their abilities and, when old, gave up only reluctantly: "My vagina is fine, yet among my people it is said of me 'it is finished with you'." (68, p. 248)

Little is known about the number of the hierodules lodged in the temples for the sake of prostitution. For some of the temples in the Near East, already under

Greco-Roman influence, the employment of thousands of hierodules has been attested, not only of females but also of males. (There is repeated evidence of the spread of paederasty in the Ancient East in later periods.) It may be assumed that the number of female slaves dedicated to the goddess was fairly high, but the later customs have retained little of the original holy ritual concerning them.

On the whole it appears as if sexual abnormalities of various kinds, remedies to prevent pregnancy, venereal diseases, etc., had not infrequently reduced sexual vigour, which was, however, of the greatest importance to man in the ancient Orient. It was the means of gaining numerous descendants and of enjoying at the same time the pleasures of love fully and unreduced. When a man met with physiological obstacles, he demanded an invigoration and stimulation of his powers, and tried to obtain this by magical invocations and ritual performances. He applied for help to the gods and exorcized the evil demons and witches whom he blamed for the impairment of the joys of love. The most diverse, often very unappetizing, ingredients taken in water or beer on an empty stomach were supposed to help. Rubbing in of oil mixed with powdered iron on the genitals or the navel were also expected to produce the so-called "lifting up of heart" which in the Sumerian-Akkadian language is used for "sexual powers." Our language hardly offers a possibility to circumscribe adequately the "lifting up of the heart" with its varied aspects, but the emphasis obviously lay on sexuality. The invocations were often recited by the female partner of the man, who spoke to him in the second person and tried to incite him to love with unambiguous words and ecstatic cries. Five, six, even twelve or fifty times he should love her; the huge strength of some animals, the mountain sheep, the mountain goat, the partridge or the wild bull, was called on to pass over into the man. Apart from quite openly and plainly stated invocations and incitations, it may also seem strange today that the magician-priest was present and that it was through his magic that the successful union of the couple was to be made possible. There was no prudishness because, as has already been mentioned repeatedly, everything concerning sex seemed natural and, therefore, decent to man in the ancient Orient. Images have been made of loving couples together with the magician-priest, as this was expected to produce a magic incitement for the "lifting up of the heart" (Ill. 19).

Moreover, one did not see any difference between gods and men in matters of love. The gods fell passionately in love with the beauties in heaven, as the young men on earth with their chosen loves. We find the same in the heaven of the gods as on the earth of men: fervent wooing to begin with, demure refusal of the too passionate suitor; and, eventually, loving agreement to make love by moonlight. When, however, the courting was not successful, then the gods, too, had to have recourse to various kinds of love-magic to win the reluctant beloved and make her submissive. If a god in love—for example the young god Enki—wanted to infatuate "the lovely young girl, who stands in the street like a garden of blossoming apple trees," he had to sprinkle her with milk from a green bowl, "so that she would run after him" (ZA NF 22, 164, 116 seq.). There were invocations "for a woman to come" (which probably means "falling in love"), or, for jealous husbands: "that the wife of a man may not lift her eyes to another man." Moreover, if an "image" of the desired woman was made of fat, the dough of bread or of clay, with her name written on it and was then buried at a special spot, then this woman would agree to make love. Stones were used to incite love, and stones to prevent love, and there also were stones to enhance and stones to prevent conception, etc.

Yet notwithstanding all the joys and pleasures which love provided for the man, he had also to pay attention to definite "rules of purity" when being with a woman, as the intimate connection with her made him "unclean" under certain circumstances. The Hittite regulations were specially strict. Officials of the temples were not allowed to undertake any service for the gods after they had enjoyed love, without taking a purifying bath, which would give back to them the required cultic purity; officials contravening this were thought to be offending the gods and deserved death. There were severe rules about purity also for the royal harems, and the "unclean" wives and concubines were strictly forbidden to approach the king (109), as we are told by the harem regulations of the mid-Assyrian kings. (112)

With this we come to the next chapter, "Harem," although we know that only a few problems have been hinted at, and have in no way been exhausted of the themes concerning "Sacred Marriage" and "Lifting up of the Heart" in the chapter we are now closing.

WOMEN RULERS AND LIFE IN THE HAREM

The life of the individual woman in the Ancient East is still rather unknown to us. The "woman of the people" formed no point of interest for the general public, her activities were confined to the family, the bringing-up of children and the household. Suddenly, as with a strong light, one or the other detail of her life is lit up, but enough material for "biographies" can hardly ever be assembled.

On the other hand, we are fairly well informed about some women rulers of the Ancient East. We come to know through various documents their often very important positions, their rights and duties and, from time to time, it is also possible to get a glimpse into a harem. It cannot exactly be stated for how long there have been harems, the "hidden places," the "unapproachables." Documents about reforms by Urukagina, dating from the middle of the 3rd millennium, mention "houses and fields of the harem." But only of a much later period, the second half of the 2nd millennium, can we get more detailed information about life in a royal harem; this we owe to the rulers themselves. Several rulers issued stringent instructions for the officials in the palace, and many of these rules concern the palace communities of the women, the duties of the palace and harem officials, etc. Beside the Hittite rulers (97), it was chiefly the Assyrian kings of the 14th–11th centuries B.C. who distinguished themselves by the invention of rules and decrees; we do not know, however, whether they used earlier prototypes. (112)

Yet all these instructions concern only a limited period—the second half of the 2nd millennium. We have therefore to use caution when applying this generally to other historical epochs. Anyway, life in the harem was not at all as "romantic" as it is generally thought to have been. The regulations were not there for the sake of the women's comfort, but for the well-being of the king, for his personal safety and the preservation of his purity according to the rules of the cult. A strict "protocol" seems to have been kept; it detailed, for example, the manner in which to announce to the king the death of anyone in the palace. The king's will was law, there was no contradicting him. A whole retinue of officials, courtiers and eunuchs stood ready to safeguard and to serve him. As we can gather from Assyrian decrees, all the employees were under the strict supervision of the *rāb ekalli*, the "Great One of the Palace," that is, the palace supervisor,

Queen Tuwarisas of Carchemish with her youngest child and a goat

who watched over them carefully, in particular with regard to service for the women. If courtiers or eunuchs had to enter the harem on the king's order—for instance, with a message or some other service—the supervisor had carefully to watch that nothing improper should happen. The young court officials, including the eunuchs, had to undergo severe and careful training with a subsequent thorough examination by a "council" of several high court officials; only then they were allowed to "enter the palace." Yet this did not ally the ruler's suspicion. Mutual control and supervision were the strict order of the king, and anyone who noticed somebody else's irregularity had at once to denounce him.

This applied first of all to all "matters concerning the women," which are frequently mentioned. The women lived, punctiliously screened from the entire world, in a building of their own inside the palace—the harem. According to rank they belonged to various groups. The official Assyrian court ceremonial names, after the son and the brother of the king, first the king's mother; then follow his wives, among whom the principal wife occupied the highest rank. One of her sons, as a rule the eldest, could claim the right of succession to the throne. If she had not borne any sons, the sons of the wives next in rank could succeed to the throne. (The rules about succession differed much in the various countries of the Ancient East. With the Hittites the king's son-in-law, that is his daughter's husband, also held the right to succession; in Elam the king was succeeded by his brother and so on.) The largest group of harem women was formed by the concubines. To them were added other women, whose charms had caught the ruler's fancy; they were not necessarily of princely blood; female charms and a pretty face were of equal value. A letter has been preserved by Kadashman-Enlil I, a Kassite king of the early 14th century B.C., to the Egyptian Pharaoh:

"When I wrote to you to marry your daughter, the answer I received said: since the earliest times Egyptian princesses have been given to no one. Why do you say this? You can do what you like. There are enough grown-up daughters and lovely women. Send me any good-looking woman you like; who would be able to say that she is not a princess?" (77, I, p.61)

Thus in the harems women of different ranks, backgrounds and ages lived together. To them were added numerous maids and female slaves, who had to serve and to entertain the ladies. It is evident that this close common life of so many women could not fail to create problems. To introduce definite rules for it must have seemed necessary to the kings; particular stress was laid again and again on an irreproachable and reserved behaviour of the courtiers and eunuchs. They were forbidden to approach any palace lady nearer than seven steps, and this only in the presence of the supervisor. It is further stated that when "a lady of the palace uses abusive language" or "quarrels with one of her equals," the young officials and the eunuchs were not allowed to stop to listen out of curiosity; this would have been considered a crime for which the offender was punished with one hundred strokes and the cutting off of one ear.

The manners of the palace ladies themselves seem not always to have been without reproach. They were reprimanded for quarrels and scuffles and for being insufficiently clothed in the presence of courtiers; and even the wives of the kings did not always behave well. It seems that they tried to solve differences with other harem ladies by using physical force: for there are regulations forbidding the "wives" to "scuffle" with the "lower-rank women" while using slanderous and blasphemous words. Rule 10 states that if they were caught in dishonourable behaviour, their "throats would be cut."

It is not surprising that in these secluded communities passions often clashed; especially as the everyday life was no doubt rather monotonous. The main occupations of the women in the harem were dancing and playing—there were always many female singers in the palace—the upbringing of the children, and female handiwork as spinning, weaving and plaiting for basket-making. Many an artistically embroidered royal garment which we see in a picture or on a sculpture, was made in the shady inner courts of the royal harems. Every little event, every interruption of the daily monotony was welcome to the women and young girls, but these, too, were sometimes forbidden: "... if men have to execute an order concerning the watering of the gardens inside the palace, and the women of the palace stop near to this place at the end of their path, this has to be reported to the inspector of the palace. He must chase them away from this end of the path." Unrelenting severity was to see to it that the women entertained no uncontrolled connections with the world outside. For certainly many a woman in

42

the palace will at one time or other have tried to establish contact, to find confidential friends inside or outside the palace, or even to escape from the harem. The suspicion of treason and conspiracy, permanently entertained by the kings, has dictated many of the rules, probably also that which forbade the harem women to make their servants presents in gold, silver or precious stones. Cases of bribery were not rare; sometimes even queens were involved, when they had tried to bribe palace officials with generous presents. (114)

Illicit intimate relations with a woman of the harem were punished with especial severity. The mere suspicion could endanger life. A Hittite document of the 14th century B.C. reports that a man had to pay with his life for having looked indecently at one of the women in the palace. (90, p.141) This report is contained in a contract, which the Hittite Great-King Shuppiluliuma signed with his new brother-in-law Chukkana of Azzi, to whom he had given his sister as wife to strengthen their political connections. But he did not omit to draw Chukkana's attention to the fact that there were different customs in the two countries, and he urged him, while at the Hittite court, to observe with meticulous care all the regulations about behaviour, especially to be well on his guard against any palace woman: "... do not go too near her, do not ever say a word to her. Nor shall your man servant, nor your maid go too near her. Beware of her. Whenever a palace woman appears, jump as far as possible out of her way, leave the path free for her." (112)

Owing to the delicate character of the intimate life in the harem, circumstantial reports about it have hardly ever been made. In connection with the story of Esther, the harem which the Persian Great-King Xerxes I (486–465 B.C.) entertained at Susa, has been described somewhat more in detail, also how the king chose his wife from among several beautiful maidens: "Now when every maid's turn was come to go in to King Ahasveros, after that she had been twelve months, according to the manner of the women (for so were the days of their purifications accomplished, to wit, six months with oil and myrrh, and six months with sweet odours, and with other things for the purifying of the women). In the evening she went, and on the morrow she returned into the second house of the women, to the custody of Shaashgas, the king's chamberlain, which kept the concubines. She came in unto the king no more, except the king

delighted in her, and that she was called by name." (Esther 2, 12–14)

In the writings of the Greek and Roman historians, too, there are from time to time hints at the life and the activities in the harems of the Persian kings. Thus Herakleides of Kyme tells us that the women in the harems slept in daytime, so as to be fresh for the night which they had to spend as concubines of the king by lamplight with singing and music. They also accompanied him when he went hunting (Fragment 1).

Worth mentioning is the "collective harem" which is said to have existed in the 9th century at the court of the Viceroy of Guzana (Tell Halaf). There the wives of the officers and officials were living together: this may have to be explained as a security measure. (66)

The king's visits certainly aroused much excitement among the women in the royal harems, and the preparations by the Assyrian and Hittite women probably resembled closely those of the Persian:

"The women are sitting on the lovely couch with the cushions; they adorn themselves with clips, with square earrings and a necklace decorated with gold: 'When will the master come to us? When will we have the pleasure of experiencing love with our bodies!'"

(Avesta, Yast. 17, 10, p. 278)

It is a pity that besides these eloquent descriptions there are no pictorial representations from the ancient oriental harems. One of the rulers of Susa, called Tempt-ahar (second half of 2nd millennium), says in an inscription in the temple of Inshushinak that he had set up beside his own statue that of his "beloved female servants;" that is, probably, of women in his harem. Unfortunately, these statues have not been preserved. All we learn of the appearance of the women by the regulations for the Assyrian harems is that their "standard" garment consisted of a skirt worn round the hips, of an (upper) garment, of shoes and of a white veil. The latter was used not only as a help in increasing their womanly charms, for the precept of "veiling" applied certainly also to the women of the palace whenever they showed themselves to the people outside. These "standard" garments, which they were allowed to take with them when travelling, were greatly refined in the course of time. In the 3rd millennium B.C., garments made of fur were still thought to be precious (Ill.8); they were even imitated, with a rough bath-towel-like material (Ill.25, 29). As the art of weaving steadily improved, fine trimmings and braids were made to decorate the edges and hems, and the simple shawl-like wraps, which left one shoulder bare (Ill. 16), were now replaced by dresses with sleeves (Ill. 13b). Subtly pleated clothes and bonnets, others richly draped, and thin veil-like fabrics became the fashion, as soon as improved weaving produced them (Ill. 13a, 48). These, as well as multi-coloured necklaces and bracelets, were worn in those early millennia by the women and young girls whenever they could afford them—the jewellery even was sometimes unbecomingly excessive (Ill. 4, 11, 46b, 82). Not only the women in the harems liked to adorn themselves with "golden necklaces;" the discoveries from burial-places and plenty of pictorial representations show that the love of jewellery was characteristic of all women in Antiquity. Doubtless, however, the women of the harem, leading a rather boring life, spent more time than others in beautifying and adorning themselves. Moreover, theirs was an economically secure existence, although they had to pay for the admittance to the "inaccessible" with the loss of all personal rights: these masses of women were "prisoners."

There was, however, one exception: the queen. The wife as well as the mother of the ruler could occupy a dominating position, partly due to their own cleverness and their special political abilities, partly also through the dignity which the throne, the mere "fact of their being the queen," had bestowed upon them. The existence of this special rank of queen can definitely be proved for the Hittite empire. There the queens occupied an "office" which comprised special political, administrative, cultic and various other rights, all quite independent of the king's office. From other areas there are no reliable sources with similar material; but it seems as if the Hittite "prototype" had not been left isolated.

Many queens became famous; the following pages will speak of them. But compared with the masses of their contemporaries it was only a small number of women who succeeded in rising to the throne, and to ruling their country independently. Queen Kubaba deserves special mention, for her career was quite an exceptional one. Her background had been the public house. Clever and resolute, she made use of a propitious occasion, in about 2573 B.C., to seat herself on the throne of Kish. She thereby founded a dynasty which retained power for about a hundred years, while she herself was entered in the list of historical sovereigns as the "beer-woman." Later on, too, one woman or another was able to accede to the throne, but most of their reigns were neither long nor of any importance. The Sassanid Queen Buran, for example, reigned hardly two years (Ill. 87); usually these queens have not become famous.

As a rule the independent political activities of the queens were confined to acting as temporary rulers for the minor heir-apparent. The most famous of these female rulers is Semiramis. She has, however, won fame not because she reigned for several years for her son who was a minor, the later King Adadnirari III, but through her "Hanging Gardens," reckoned already in Antiquity as one of the "Seven Wonders of the World." But the queer thing is that the fame of the "Hanging Gardens" was mistakenly ascribed to her. Semiramis/Sammuramāt ("Mistress of the Palace") was the wife of Shamshi-Adad V (824–810 B.C.), and evidently was so important a personality that soon after her death truth and legend were interwoven and she was herself connected with this "Wonder of the World," the luxurious green and flowering terraced gardens, which really should be ascribed to Nebuchadnezzar (604–562 B.C.). He had them laid out for his Median wife Amytis, and arranged for them to be watered by an ingenious and elaborate system, bringing the water up to all the terraces, so as to imitate by a magnificent lay-out the hills and trees of her Median home and to cure her of her homesickness. Of the historical Queen Semiramis/Sammuramāt, whose home was Babylon, we still do not know very much, notwithstanding her legendary fame. It is, however, remarkable that in Ashur among the large stelae of the great Assyrian kings there is also one of her with the following inscription:

"Stela of Sammuramāt,

The mistress of the palace of Shamshi-Adad,

Of the king of the World, king of Assyria;

The Mother of Adadniraris,

The king of the World, king of Assyria,

Of (...) of Salmanassar,

King of the four Corners of the World." (73)

She is the only female ruler in this row of "male" stelae—an outstanding testimony to her importance as an energetic regent. She has, as she proclaimed, "set herself proudly on the throne of the kings," so as to take charge of the fate of Assyria. Herodotus reports of her "that she

44

had these marvellous dikes built in the lowlands where the stream previously used to turn the whole country into a vast sea" (I, 184). She evidently did a great deal for the irrigation of the country. Soon she was surrounded by myths and legends. So she was believed to have been transformed into a dove after death; to have killed all her lovers as soon as she had been united to them in love; she also was said to have erected strange and wonderful buildings and to have led adventurous campaigns as far as India, taking with her, so as to frighten the Indians, thousands of stuffed black bulls, pretending them to be "elephants." It may also be thought of interest that she is reported to have invented on her military expeditions a garment "which made it difficult to see whether the person wearing it was a man or a woman;" this garment—the trousers—was, as Diodorus reports (Book II, 6), so "pleasant" that the Persians, and later the Medians, took over its use. Eventually, apart from the invention of this "pleasant" garment which is still worn today, she was supposed to have been responsible also for the seventh "Wonder of the World," the Hanging Gardens, while her true historical image has been more and more embellished and glossed over. (73) Yet she was certainly one of the great personalities of Antiquity.

She was not the only Assyrian queen who gained for herself a name by her political activities. About seventy years after Sammuramāt, there appears another female ruler who, like her, proved herself a master in the pursuit of the affairs of the state: this was Naqi'a, the wife of Sennacherib (704–681 B.C.), mother of Esarhaddon (680–669 B.C.) and grandmother of Ashurbanipal (668–626 B.C.). The way this determined and ambitious, and highly intelligent lady "managed" her son Esarhaddon and, after his death, already a grandmother, her grandson Ashurbanipal, calls for the greatest admiration. Originally she seems to have held merely the place of a concubine of Sennacherib; she succeeded, however, in having Esarhaddon, her son, proclaimed crown-prince instead of Arad-Ninlil who was already heir-apparent, and she herself moved up to the highest rank among the wives of Sennacherib. The promotion of her son Esarhaddon was not devoid of far-reaching political consequences. The Assyrian party of the injured stepbrothers murdered Sennacherib, the father, and rose in revolt against the favoured Esarhaddon. There followed a bloody fratricidal war, but Esarhaddon was able to bring it to a

victorious end; not, however, without the help of his mother, who, probably, was a Babylonian of Aramaic origin. Thus the Babylonian party had won against the Assyrian. Naqi'a once more interfered in "high politics." After the death of Esarhaddon she supported (passing over the elder one) the younger of his sons on the throne: Ashurbanipal, who originally had been designated for the priesthood. Even when she was a grandmother she was still disposed to fight and it was dangerous to provoke her anger. When Ashurbanipal became king she demanded of the officials und dignitaries:

"As from today, if anyone speaks badly of Ashurbanipal, and you do not come to me and inform Zakūtu, his grandmother (Zakūtu was her Assyrian name), and Ashurbanipal, your lord, or when you hear of plans to kill or murder Ashurbanipal, and you do not come to me ... or when, should a criminal try intriguing against Ashurbanipal or me, you do not come to me and inform Zakūtu and Ashurbanipal, then ..."

(77, I, p. 74 seq.)

Naqi'a was a great and most energetic ruler, who played for many decades an outstanding role in both the internal and the general politics of the court. She had a court of her own and even spoke of her own "reign." Her son Esarhaddon had represented himself together with her on a bronze tablet, which certainly was most unusual as an official representation and has to be taken as a sign of the great esteem in which the king held his mother (Ill. 62). At the same time this also illustrates the importance of the post of "King-Mother" to which we shall come back later.

Incidentally, Ashurbanipal, the grandson of Naqi'a, also seems to have had a wife who presided with dignity in the palace as its female ruler; her picture has been preserved in one of the most beautiful reliefs of the Ancient East (Ill. 70).

It depended to a great extent on the intelligence and cleverness of the queen whether she was able not only to attend to her ritual, representative and administrative duties as the "first lady of the harem," but also to assist the ruler in the affairs of the state, especially when he was away from the capital. Highly informative in this respect is the correspondence of a queen of Mari, which French excavators discovered in the course of the clearance of the royal palace of that town. The kingdom of Mari, to the west of Assyria, on the upper reaches of the

Euphrates, was chiefly under its ruler Zimrilim (1716–1695 B.C.) of great cultural and political importance. Zimrilim himself was at first one of the allies and later one of the great enemies of Hammurabi of Babylon, to whose plans of expanding his rule, the kingdom of Mari formed an obstacle. Of the four wives of Zimrilim, whose names we know, Shibtu, queen of Mari, was his principal wife. Her correspondence is of outstanding importance in showing us her position at the court, and of interest, too, with regard to many another queen of similar rank, whose everyday duties may have been much like hers. Her correspondence deserves, therefore, a fairly thorough study. (3) High officials of the king appealed to the queen not only in administrative concerns, but informed her also about political and military matters of importance: for example about the situation on the borders of Mari, as explored by the frontier guards, and about the movements of an army of 1500 men on the banks of the Tigris. One of the governors reported to her that he had been successful in the political-military work entrusted to him as "peace-maker," and that "peace and friendly relations" were now re-established with the districts north of Mari.

The king entrusted his wife even with the organization of particularly difficult and "confidential" undertakings, as he probably could rely on her secrecy and her ability in negotiations, and because she was a woman "with whom one could steal horses." Thus, she was once asked to choose reliable men able to do some "special jobs": they had to collect from a certain place in an administrative building—probably a kind of embassy—containers of "slabs," written documents, and to bring them to Mari. We learn by a letter from the queen to her husband that this diplomatic, evidently "most secret" enterprise was successful and that the slabs were now in her safe-keeping.

But apart from these duties, which no doubt were of some importance for political and military affairs, the queen, according to the extant letters and reports, had to fulfil quite a number of other tasks. Inhabitants of the town and members of the court used to appeal to her in specially equivocal situations, asking for her help or intervention: for example, asking her to use her influence for the release of some women from imprisonment for debt; or she was asked to intervene in a libel affair connected with a burglary, and once she even approached the governor of a neighbouring town with regard to the "love affair" of a certain lady in a town of the vicinity. Her exalted husband, too, had numerous commissions for her. Yet their personal letters also show the mutual and sincere sympathy which united Zimrilim and Shibtu. She consulted omens when he was away at war, and implored him to pay attention to the relevant portent so that he might return "safely and healthy and with a happy mind" to Mari. She sent him clothes which she had made herself and asked him to wear them, and when she had borne twins, her first thought was for her husband: "I have this moment borne a small couple of twins, a son and a daughter. May my lord rejoice!" While on his tours of inspection or at war campaigns, which he had to undertake to safeguard his frontiers towards Ashur and mainly those towards Babylon, the king was always in contact with his wife, informed her about his health, confirmed happily that the auspicious omen had been fulfilled and asked for news from the palace of Mari. As he seems to have been much concerned with the "house of the containers of wine", his wine cellar, he gave advice about wine to the queen in several letters. He begged her to supervise personally the filling of the barrels with the costly imported wines, for example with those which came from Aleppo, giving particular attention to the "red wine," which evidently was thought of as specially precious. He also asked her earnestly to see to it that the wines were sent quickly to the great Hammurabi of Babylon, at that time his ally. Not much later, when their alliance had been broken, this same king overthrew Zimrilim and annihilated him, while the town and palace of Mari—including the wine cellar—were completely destroyed. In the ruins of the once magnificent and prosperous palace there have lately been discovered many finds of valuable and precious works of art (Ill. 29, 32), and now, after 2600 years, the correspondence of its remarkable queen has also been saved. (3)

We now have to examine the position of the Hittite queen comparing it with that of the Mesopotamian queen. In Chatti, a country on the banks of the river Halys to the north-west of Assyria, there existed a peculiar attitude with regard to the "throne of the queenship," whereby the queen gradually came to occupy a position almost equal to that of the king. This is most evident in the status of Queen Puduchepa, of whom more

46

will have to be said. The original country of Chatti, ruled by energetic leaders, had developed in the course of centuries to an important realm, whose kings called themselves Great-Kings and reigned according to the absolute despotism of the Ancient Orient. Yet Hittite royalty was somewhat different from the Babylonian-Assyrian, in that the king after his death was raised to be a god and was worshipped with religious sacrifices. Consequently, the king's death was proclaimed with the formula "He became God." Unfortunately it has not been proved conclusively whether the queen, too, was deified after her death, but it is at least known that sacrifices were made also to her. More significant, however, for the queen's position is the dignity, evidently inherent, in the Hittite queenship. Kingship and queenship were traced back to the earliest ancestors of the royal dynasty, and the reigning couple bore titles deduced from the names of these ancestors: the king the title "tabarna," the queen "tawananna." The queenship of the bearer of this title was inviolable and could not be taken from her, even when she survived her husband. The wife of the next ruler, usually her daughter-in-law, could succeed to the rights of the old tawananna only after the latter's death; until then she was only called "wife of the king." (29)

Originally the succession followed the female line. Only after much fighting for the right to inherit the throne and after internal strife, King Telepinu (approx. 1525 B.C.) could establish a patriarchal rule of succession. Yet the Hittite queen was evidently able to retain an independent and highly influential position. With the accession to the "throne of queenship," which Tawananna, the earliest ancestor, had handed down from the oldest times from queen to queen, she gained an authoritative office which supplied her with extensive rights.

The most impressive figure of a woman on the Hittite throne was Puduchepa. She has always been considered the Near Eastern queen, who enjoyed the greatest independence at the side of the king and has been recognized also "internationally" as equal to him. She was the wife of Hattusilis III (1289–1265 B.C.), one of the most important rulers of the younger Hittite kingdoms. We have comparatively more details about her origin, as her husband himself has recorded it in his "autobiography." She was the daughter of a priest from Kummanni in Kizzuwatna (to the north of Cyprus on the Asiatic mainland) and had herself been a priestess; her name signifies

"servant of the goddess Chepa." Her husband Hattusilis, who was also a former priest, married her on his return from Egypt, where he had accompanied his then still reigning brother Muwatalli as military commander. As he wrote, the marriage was "ordered by the deity," yet love also seems not to have been absent, as he continues his account: "We lived in matrimonial union and the deity granted us the love of husband and wife and we had sons and daughters." (90, p. 160)

At the side of her husband, Puduchepa played an active role in the political affairs of the state. The Egyptian Pharaoh Rameses II, with whom Hattusilis had concluded a peace treaty after the battle of Kadesh, addressed his letters not only to his Hittite "brother," but in almost the same form to the latter's wife, who then on her part sent him the relevant answers. The Hittite specimen of the peace treaty between the two countries, inscribed on a silver tablet, shows on the front the seal of Hattusilis and on the back that of Puduchepa. At the occasion of the signing of this document, she exchanged letters of congratulation with the Egyptian queen; besides this some more "international" correspondence of hers has been preserved. Nearly all documents from Hattusilis are composed also in the name of his wife; she also shared with the king his decisions concerning internal as well as external politics. She had to perform representative religious duties and seems to have been in charge of the administration of the palace. As we learn from some documents, she retained her high rank as tawananna as the king's mother after the death of her husband. Puduchepa certainly was qualified for her high office by a marked political talent and, moreover, as a former priestess, was a woman of outstanding education and intelligence. She even seems to have been interested in clay tablets, as she had such tablets from Kizzuwatna, her home country, collected and copied.

Owing to the kind of sources at our disposal, we lack equally vivid pictures of other Hittite queens, yet a family scandal in the royal dynasty, which caused a fair amount of sensation, provides us with interesting information about a tawananna, this time a queen mother. Chinti, the wife of Suppiluliumas (1380–1346 B.C.), had survived her husband when he became "god," and created various difficulties for her stepson Mursilis II (1345–1315 B.C.)—who, by the way, was the father of Hattusilis and thereby the father-in-law of Puduchepa.

This induced him to prosecute her and to "depose" her as tawananna. His "accusation" submitted to the gods contained the following weighty charges:

"When my father had become god, Arnuwanda, my brother, and I caused no harm to the tawananna nor did we disparage her. In the way she had administered the palace and the country of Chatti in my father's time, thus she went on in the time of my brother. When my brother had become god, I too caused no harm to the tawananna, nor have I disparaged her . . . Do you not see, oh gods, how she has handed over everything from my father's house to the temple of the dead and to the mausoleum? And of all that she had brought from Babylon, she made gifts for the whole population in Chattusha, and she saved nothing."

(90, p. 150 seq.)

He also accused her of having collected tribute behind the back of the king and ruined the house of Suppiluliumas in every possible way. He made her responsible for Mursilis' speech defect and even accused her of having occasioned the death of his wife, because the old tawananna had cursed her before the gods.

Apart from these accusations, this text tells us that the queen mother was in charge of the administration of the palace and of the country of Chatti. She had far-reaching administrative powers and probably even the right to collect tributes. Yet, owing to the regulations for the succession to the throne, valid in the Hittite empire, the tawananna had less influence on the designation of the heir apparent than, for example, Assyrian queens, who possibly had a voice in the deliberations or at least tried to have one. The pertinent facts about the queen mother, Naqi'a, have been described above. Several other queen mothers have taken up arms for their sons and have helped them to the throne. The Ugarit Queen Achatmilku (13th century B.C.), for instance, intervened after the death of her husband Niqmepa very energetically to secure the succession for her younger son Ammistamru II., and even banished two elder sons to Cyprus, whose rights she disregarded. (13)

In many areas of the Ancient East, therefore, the queen mother occupied positions of considerable might. If, however, she was in disagreement with the king on internal politics, serious discord could disrupt the royal family, and the queen mother be removed from her office. The legal proceedings started by Mursilis against

the tawananna, monstrous as they were, were not an isolated instance: Danuchepa, the wife of Muwatalli, was probably treated by her stepson Urchiteshup (1297–1290 B.C.) in quite the same way as Tawananna Chinti. It is further worth mentioning that the annals of the Israelite kings of the 9th century B.C. report a similar case: Asa, the King of Judah, "removed Maacha his mother . . . from being queen" (I Kings, 15/13).

On the other hand, it is interesting to read in an Ugaritic text about the "nomination" of a queen mother, or rather of forbidding her nomination. An important document from the time of Ammistamru II (13th century B.C.) deals with the divorce of Ammistamru from his wife, and then proceeds to forbid the crown-prince strictly to make his mother, the divorced wife of Ammistamru, "queen mother" in Ugarit. If, however, he did so, he would have to lay his garment on the throne and go wherever he wanted to go; that is, he himself would lose the throne by the illegal "nomination" of his mother as queen mother. (88, p. 126 seq.)

In Elam, too, the country to the east of Babylon, some queens and queen mothers deserve mention as influential and outstanding rulers. The ancestress of the Epartides, known as "Silhahas' Sister" and "Blessed Mother" (amma hashduk), is one of the few queens enjoying complete independence as a ruler (approx. 1800 B.C.). Of later periods Napir-asu (approx. 1250 B.C.) (Ill. 48) and especially Nahhunte-utu (the mother of little Bar-Uli) must not be forgotten. As in Elam the levirate and marriages between brothers and sisters were customary, this queen became the wife of two of her brothers, first of Kutir-Nahhunte and later of Shilhak-Inshushinak (12th century B.C.). Nor ought we to omit from the list of famous queens of the Ancient East, Baranamtarra (11), wife of Lugalanda of Lagash (approximately 2400 B.C.), who was efficient in business, or Adad-guppi, the mother of the Babylonian King Nabonidus (555–538 B.C.). Although she may not have been a priestess of the moon god Sin of Charran (there is no definite evidence of this), yet she was his devout worshipper, and all through her long life thoroughly influenced her son's policy particularly with regard to religion. She was said to have lived to the age of 104, when she died in the year 547 B.C. A great "lamentation was organized" after her death, and she was honoured by the country going into mourning for seven days. (28, 93)

48

If it were not for the regrettable lack of space, one could illustrate the position and importance of the queens and queen mothers by quoting more instances—also from the history of Israel, in which several female rulers played rather inglorious, even bloody roles (see for example 2 Kings, 11).

After these reports on the queens, some account should be given of princesses, the daughters of kings. Like the princes, they were carefully educated, and when adult, frequently took up influential positions in the service of the temples. Close connections between temple and palace were of use to the sovereign, as this offered him the chance of increasing his influence on the priests. The priesthood as a career was, therefore, often greatly welcomed by male or female members of the dynasty.

But many princesses were given further, often politically still more effective duties: they were sent to the harems of foreign rulers to promote, by the marriage between members of the two dynasties, a close and friendly association of their countries. In all the Near East there was frequent recourse to this custom. It seems, however, that it sometimes was the "greed for gold" which induced the father to give his daughter away in exchange for the valuable metal; this can especially be deduced from letters by Kassite rulers to Egyptian Pharaohs of the Amarna period. Yet there were also instances of kings who agreed only after repeated requests to give away their daughters. The Egyptian Pharaoh Thutmose IV is said to have offered seven times until

Artatama, the Mitanni king, gave him one of his daughters. A young daughter of Hattusilis and Puduhepa also went to Egypt. To seal the peace treaty between her father and the Pharaoh Rameses II she was married to the latter in the thirty-fourth year of his reign, when he was at least a man of fifty. Rameses made the Hittite princess his principal wife and gave her the Egyptian name of "Truth is the Beauty of the Rē." It is further reported that yet another Hittite princess was sent with rich presents to the harem of Rameses II. (90, p. 163) Anyway, these alliances contributed to the peaceful connection which lasted for decades between the two countries.

One more Hittite princess became known because of the special event which brought about her marriage with Mattiwaza of Mitanni—and because this is mentioned in the peace treaty between the two rulers. Mattiwaza was originally an independent king of Mitanni, but had embarked on a war with the mighty Hittite King Suppiluliumas (1380–1346 B.C.), and lost his country with its capital, Washukanni. The enemy armies killed and ravaged Mitanni. Mattiwaza was forced to flee, and in his distress sought refuge "in the lion's den," that is, with Suppiluliumas himself who received him graciously and reinstalled him as a kind of vassal in his own, though now considerably diminished, Mitanni realm. Mitanni was of importance to the Hittites as a bulwark against Assyria. Mattiwaza reports about the benefits granted to him by his new master: "And I, Mattiwaza, the son of a king, when I went to the great king, then I had with me three chariots, two Churri people and two guardsmen, only the garment I was wearing and nothing else. And the great king had mercy on me and gave me chariots covered with gold, horses, gear, ... two jugs of silver and gold with beakers of silver and gold ... a magnificent garment, all this and jewellery, all one could think of, all this he gave me ..." (84, p. 343) Moreover, King Suppiluliumas gave him his daughter as wife. But he made the following contract with him:

"... If you, Mattiwaza, son of a king, and you, people of Churri, do not abide by the words of this contract—then may the gods, who watch over the oaths, destroy you, Mattiwaza, and you, people of Churri, together with your country, your wives and your goods ... As one cannot grow plants on a field covered with salt, so you, Mattiwaza, should you take another wife, and you, people of Churri, with your wives, your sons and your country shall have no descendants. May the gods wipe off the earth your name and the seed of your second wife, should you take one ..." (29, p. 154)

By this contract the Great-King Suppiluliumas forbade Mattiwaza to take any other woman as his "wife," apart from the Hittite princess, although this probably did not apply to "concubines." However that may be, the contract shows how far the political importance of the presumptive father—or son-in-law—formed the basis for any arrangement by which a princess was to be given (or not to be given) in marriage. Suppiluliumas is responsible also for another dynastic marriage, that of his sister with the ruler of Azzi, whom—as we reported above—he urged to observe the Hittite rules concerning his behaviour in the presence of the palace women. He himself married the Babylonian princess whom later her stepson Mursilis was to "depose" as tawananna. Esarhaddon, too, already mentioned, gave one of his daughters in marriage abroad. An unlucky political situation and the threat to his frontiers to the north and northeast induced him to send her to the harem even of a nomad ruler, a "barbarian," Bartatua (Greek: Protothyas), a prince of the Scythians. But he hesitated owing to scruples, and, worried as he was, he applied to the sun god:

"If Esarhaddon, the king of Assyria, has given a princess to Bartatua as his wife, will then Bartatua, the king of the land of the Scythians, speak to Esarhaddon, king of Assyria, true and inviolable words of concord and observe the oath of allegiance which he swore to Esarhaddon, and will he do all that is good for Esarhaddon?"

(Klauber, *Politisch-religiöse Texte aus der Sargonidenzeit*, 1913, p. 29)

Whatever the sun god's answer, the treaty was concluded, but brought Esarhaddon only temporary security, unable to prevent the loss of Media: the daughter was sent on the long journey to the "barbarians." The sending abroad of a princess often occasioned heavy expenses. Not only abundant provisions had to be collected for the long journey, many jugs of oil, butter, cream, sourmilk, beer, etc., but also a large amount of costly presents, and besides there were the numerous servants who had to accompany their young mistress. A princess from Mitanni was said to have arrived in her new home with 317 female slaves.

It can be guessed from this that the harems of oriental despots contained the most diverse elements, especially as from time to time pretty slaves from abroad were added as "presents." It is, for instance, recorded that the Parthian King Phraates IV received as such an "attention" from the Roman Caesar Augustus a lovely Italian slave, called Musa. The king made her his wife and she became the mother of his successor Phraates V (2 B.C.–4 A.D.), whom she herself is said to have married after the death of her husband (marriages between near blood-relations were admissible at that time).

Female slaves in great numbers probably arrived in the harems from abroad when it had been possible to capture the harem of the enemy king in war—a particular satisfaction for the victor and an added shame for the vanquished. The kings, therefore, never omitted to record these heroic feats in their annals of war. Shilhak-Inshushinak, the king of Elam (1150–1120 B.C.), writes after a successful campaign, through which he had got hold of the town of Karindash: "All the descendants of the king of Karindash, his wives, concubines and relatives were rounded up and taken into exile ..." (45, p. 110) But the kings of Elam were not any luckier. Ashurbanipal made Elam into a desert and reported:

"... on the fields I sowed salt and thistles. The daughters and wives of the kings of Elam, of the old and the young generations, the town bailiffs, the commanders, all officers including the technicians, and all inhabitants, whether men or women, big or small ... all these I drove away as booty to Assyria ..." (45, p. 131)

And in 671 B.C., Esarhaddon even took the harem of the Ethiopian King Taharka to Assyria.

It is, however, evident that, inversely, the rulers who conquered the Near East, also tried to collect such valuable "booty." The Egyptian Pharaoh Amenophis II (1448–1422 B.C.) carried away to Egypt, among others, 232 sons and 323 daughters of princes, 270 female court singers and thousands of other inhabitants of Palestine. (74, p. 188) The Persian Great-King, Darius III, was humiliated in a similar manner by Alexander the Great. During his victorious campaign Alexander succeeded in capturing the king's harem in Syria. It was not unusual for rulers to be accompanied on their campaigns or travels by harem women. The Assyrian rules for harems, mentioned above, contain the king's orders for such travels of the harem women. But the train of women which Darius took with him on his campaign has certainly by far out-numbered that of any of his ancestors. Q. Curtius Rufus, the Roman historian, has given a detailed description of the capture of the great-king's harem in his *History of Alexander the Great*. According to him, the troops of Darius were followed by Sisigambis, the king's mother, on a car, on another his wife; the women, accompanying the queens, were on horseback. Then followed fifteen so-called travelling carriages, on which were the king's children with their governesses and a crowd of eunuchs, ... then came, on more carriages, 365 concubines of the king, also magnificently dressed and adorned" (*Historiarum Alexandri Magni*, III, 3). This harem was at Alexander's mercy; Darius offered in vain an immense ransom. The harem was taken to the royal palace at Susa. Darius came to a miserable end; fleeing in far-off East Asia, he was killed by a murderer, while Alexander conquered a huge empire and strove now as "Persian Great-King" for the domination of the world. To secure the union of the Macedonians and Persians, to "fuse" them, he conceived the plan of a "mass marriage" of Macedonian men with Persian women. He was said to have distributed to at least ten thousand Macedonians wedding presents on this "happy occasion." He himself married Stateira, the daughter of the last Persian Great-King. (82, p. 303) According to Q. Curtius Rufus, he took pleasure in some oriental customs and had a harem laid out for himself:

"365 concubines, the same number as Darius had entertained, filled his palace, and there were quite a number of eunuchs accustomed to be used like women."   (*Historiarum Alexandri Magni*, VI, 6)

In conclusion it has to be stated that the "custom of the harem" increased more and more in the course of time. The Assyrian shadow-king, Ninurta-tukul-Ashur (12th century B.C.), still entertained a comparatively small harem of approximately forty women; that of the Sassanid King Khosrau I (531–579 A.D.), with allegedly twelve thousand young girls and women, was no doubt one of the largest. It seems that the rulers sometimes even met with difficulties in accommodating these large numbers of women. The buildings of some harems had to be enlarged, others to be replaced by larger ones. Hundreds, even thousands of women were in this way "imprisoned" for the benefit of a single man and sequestered from any other marriage. The same happened to the women and young girls in the smaller harems of the wealthy upper layer of society. All these women were excluded from the social life of the community and were in fact not free persons. There are several hints indicating that among some parts of the population, this led to a scarcity of women and to additional poverty, so that women were even lent out for temporary marriages. In the epoch of the Sassanids the "imprisonment" of women and their lack of rights reached its apex. In the 6th century A.D., there was a kind of revolution in the Sassanid empire with a leader of the name of Mazdak, which turned against the rich nobility, the "luxury of the mighty," and demanded equal conditions for the poor and the rich; also a new distribution of houses and goods, and, simultaneously, a "distribution of the women." (87, p. 140 seq.; 9, p. 166)

The liberation of the women and young girls from the harem and a "distribution" would, in fact, have brought about an improvement of their legal and social position, as a further deterioration simply would have been impossible. These revolutionary endeavours were defeated by the nobility, and Mazdak himself and thousands of his followers were killed. The women of the Near East remained for several more centuries in a state of dependence with reduced social and personal rights, as Islam, too, brought about no fundamental change. Only in the most recent past more progressive forces in the young states of the Near East have been able to do away with old and outlived conditions, thereby bringing about a general change also in the life of women.

"MY MOUTH MAKES ME COMPARABLE WITH MEN"

The pages of this book have frequently had to report that the woman had no rights equal to those enjoyed by men. She was thought of lesser value, her position was weaker, in the family as well as in society; she was, for example, paid less for her work, etc. The question now arises whether the woman of the Ancient East accepted this position as unchangeable, as ordained by the gods, or whether she consciously and actively took up the fight for "equal rights," for a better life and greater freedom. The lack of freedom does not, of course, necessarily point to the lack of endeavours to gain it. On the contrary, there can be no doubt that the woman of the Ancient East tried to improve her life, that she learned and worked so as to get on. She did not pass the time away in idleness, but acquired learning and knowledge, "sat down to learn." This applies not only to her activities in handicraft—as the talented master of the art of spinning and weaving that she was, her products even being exported to foreign countries—but also to those of her mental capacities. Thus, she won for herself a place in one of the most respected and difficult professions, that of the scribe, usually the domain of men. She devoted to it much energy and many years of study. Yet she was not esteemed so much as a male scribe and the Assyrian King Ashurbanipal thought it necessary to apologize to the deity for having used a female scribe when asking for an oracle: "Forgive that a woman has written this and submitted it to you." (77, I, p. 387)

In fact, we know of many women who acquired the art of writing and thereby a large part of contemporary knowledge, a proof that they could carry out the same work as any man. We do not, however, intend to speak again of the differences in the position and the work of men and women, which have been described in the previous chapters, and only want to point in what we say, to the different evaluation of their work. This leads to the interesting problem, whether and in how far women were conscious of this unwarranted underestimation; there are various pieces of evidence to be considered.

The ancient oriental proverbs are very telling. In the Near East the desire for liberation from need and various hindrances has often taken the form only of an indirect criticism. Individual fate was lamented in elegies and other literary work, and a profound pessimism expressed the view that all striving was in vain and that nothing could be done against the will of the gods. Or man looked back to a paradisiacal past which, however, was lost without hope, while the present offered nothing but bitterness and hopelessness. But beside these there are many other sayings which show that human beings were not satisfied with this negative attitude, but which make it known that it is left to them to influence their own fate; by their deeds, by an active attitude to their surroundings they can bring about a change. To achieve anything, to progress man must apply effort and pain. The ancient oriental proverb, "Without efforts man will not gain anything," puts this belief into words. In this proverb man stands in the foreground; he himself decides and acts and does not wait for the gods to act. The woman, too, of the Ancient East was intelligent enough to understand this. First of all she understood that knowledge means "power." In the old oriental "Wisdom Literature" there is a sentence in the Emesal dialect, therefore probably written by a woman: "My mouth makes me comparable with men." (68, p. 238) The notion underlying this proverb is that the only woman who can progress and acquire in the family and in society a position comparable to that of man, is the woman who "strives and toils," works to improve and educate herself, is active and, seeing things clearly, acts consciously. Every woman, who had overstepped her former limitations and had got on by her own activity, could stimulate other members of her sex and strengthen their confidence in themselves. A clever and intelligent queen, a perfect weaver, a scribe who had given proof that she could play her part as well as a man even in this "man's profession," in fact every woman who in her own sphere had achieved something unusual, was a kind of pioneer for women's progress. She could be an instance of what a woman could do. A young girl, too, who succeeded in having added to her marriage contract some clauses guaranteeing her more freedom at the side of her husband, or a wife who could bind her husband not to take concubines, a bride who criticized the "bargaining" of her father and her bridegroom about the amount of the dowry, a female slave who on her own gained freedom— all of these and many more are proof for us that the women of the Ancient East strove for a change in humiliating customs and conditions. The social conditions offered them only slight chances, and their individual activities brought about no general changes. Yet women realized that inactivity and lack of personal initiative in any event led to a regress, a fall into still worse dependence. On the other hand, knowledge and energy could become an inciting influence. Women of all social layers—the female ruler and the slave, the priestess, the scribe, the skilled worker—they all have made use of the old oriental proverbial wisdom of the necessity of striving and of working to improve oneself. They may have ignored, however, that by their work and their endeavours they also contributed to the advance of society. But they certainly did so and thereby helped to mould the civilization of the Ancient East.

CHRONOLOGICAL TABLE

(The dating up to 539 B.C. is based on that used by Moortgat, *Geschichte Vorderasiens,* 1950)

Date	Political History		Civilization	Documents
approx. 100 000 to 75 000			Barda Balka: pebbles as tools	
approx. 60 000 to 40 000			Shanidar: similar to Neandertal	
approx. 35 000 to 9000			Paleolithic Mesolithic Neolithic	
approx. 9000			Incipient cultivation and domestication	
approx. 6750			Jarmo: earliest agricultural settlements	
approx. 6500 to 5700			Catalhuyuk: "preceramic" villages, numerous sites reserved for religious observances; representations of the "Great Mother"	
6th/4th millennium			Hassuna-Samarra-Halaf Ubaid: multi-coloured ceramics, female clay figurines	
approx. 3000	*Uruk Period*	Earliest civic communities, particularly evident by findings in the town of Uruk	Invention of cuneiform writing and cylinder seals, monumental temple buildings	Pictographic documents
approx. 2800 to 2700	*Jamdat-Nasr Period*	Sumerian city states	Art of working metal, potter's wheel, plough, loom	Earliest administrative documents in Sumerian language
approx. 2600 to 2350	*Early Dynastic Period*	Several important city states in Mesopotamia (Ur, Lagash, Mari) Temple-and-palace communities Sharp social contrasts Lugalanda of Lagash (wife Baranamtarra) Urukagina of Lagash, reformer	Royal graves of Ur	Inscriptions by kings, contracts, administrative documents Reports on the so-called social reforms of Urukagina
approx. 2350 to 2150	*Akkad Period* First Semitic empire under Sargon of Akkad from Persian Gulf to Mediterranean, conquest of Elam Other rulers: Rimush, Naramsin		Masterpieces of sculpture and glyptics, far-reaching trade connections (India!) Priestess: Encheduanna (daughter of Sargon?)	
approx. 2150 to 2050	*Period of the Guti*	Domination by the mountain tribe of the Guti, who were expelled after a hundred years' reign	Cultural decline	

Date	Political History		Civilization	Documents
approx. 2050		Priest-king Gudea of Lagash	Flowering and hegemony of the city state of Lagash (comprising about 160,000 hectares, 17 larger, 8 smaller towns and at least 40 villages)	Numerous inscriptions and hymns
approx. 2050 to 1950	*Third Dynasty of Ur*	Urnammu, up to today the earliest known legislator	Restoration and last flowering of Sumerian civilization	"Codex Urnammu," several smaller legal texts, many documents from law-courts, contracts, protocols concerning family and matrimonial law, claims against individual slavery
		Other kings: Shulgi, Shu-Sin, Ibbi-Sin	The kings of this dynasty acted as bridegrooms at the "Sacred Marriages"	Hymns for "Sacred Marriage"
approx. 1950 to 1698	*Dynasties of Isin and Larsa*	Hegemony of the towns Isin and Larsa Kings: Iddin-Dagan, Lipit-Ishtar, Urninurta, Rimsin	"Sacred Marriage"	"Codex Lipit-Ishtar", law codex of Eshnunna in Akkadian language
approx. 1850 to 1680	*Old-Assyrian Period*	Important ruler: Shamshi-Adad I (1749–1717)	Assyrian merchant colonies in Asia Minor	Correspondence of Assyrian merchants from Kültepe (Asia Minor)
2nd half of 16th century	In Syria and Upper Mesopotamia the Churrits gained power, political union in the kingdom of *Mitanni*	Kings: Artatama I Tushratta Mattiwaza		Documents from Nuzi Contract of Suppululiumas with Mattiwaza
approx. 1370	Collapse of the kingdom of Mitanni			
approx. 1830 to 1530	*First Dynasty of Babylon* In North Mesopotamia: city state of Mari, flourishing trade centre with magnificent palace, its about 260 rooms and court-yards were thought a remarkable sight Outstanding rulers: Zimrilim (1716–1695) (wife Shibtu), other small kingdoms in the Syrian region	6th king of the First dynasty: Hammurabi (1728–1686), established a large empire from Gulf of Persia to the Syrian desert in the north, overthrew Rimsin of Larsa and Zimrilim of Mari His successors: Samsuiluna (1685–1648) Abi-eshukh (1647–1620)	Very lively small works of art, especially terracottas and seals, specially rich finds from Mari, among which were wall paintings and larger sculpture	"Codex Hammurabi," stela, 2.25 m high, with law code, documents of the nadiātum priestesses in Sippar, old-Babylonian version of "Gilgamesh Epic;" in Mari: large archive of letters
approx. 1830 to 1800	*In Elam:* Silhaha and "Silhaha's sister," ancestress of the dynasty of the "Blessed Mother"			

Date	Political History		Civilization	Documents
approx. 1530 to 1160	*Kassite Period*	Tribes from the Zagros mountains rule in Babylonia, lively diplomatic and trade connections with other countries, especially Egypt		Selective collection of Sumerian-Akkadian litera- ture, final version of the "Gilgamesh Epic"
		Kadashman-Enlil I (14th century)		Correspondence with Egyptian Pharaoh (Amarna Archive, Egypt, which contains the Egyptian correspondence with the
		Melishipak (approx. 1191–1177)	Boundary stone with representation of the king and his daughter	courts of the Near East at the time of Amenophis III and IV)
1380 to 1080	*Mid-Assyrian Period*	The Assyrians again becoming more powerful		Rules for harems by mid- Assyrian kings (14th–11th centuries)
	Elam:			
1275 to 1240	Untash-napirisha (wife Napir-asu)		Bronze statue of queen Napir-asu	Inscriptions on stelae, statues, etc.
1207 to 1171	Shutruk-Nahhunte I			
1170 to 1166	Kutir-Nahhunte I			
1165 to 1151	Shilhak-Inshushinak (wife Nahhunte-utu)		Representation of king with his daughter on a pearl	
	Hittite Period			
17th/16th century	Older Empire			Archives of clay slabs and libraries of Boghazköy
15th/12th century	Younger Empire		Reliefs on orthostats	Hittite collection of law codes
	Hittite rule in Mitanni and Syria (for example in Carchemish, Ugarit) Suppuluiumas (1380–1346)			Treaties with vassals, dynastic marriages, contract with Mattiwaza of Mitanni
	Mursilis II (1345–1315) Muwatallis (1315–1290) Battle of Kadesh Hattusilis III (1282–1250) (wife Puduchepa)			Peace treaty with Egypt, approx. 1270
	Tudhalyas IV (1250–1220)			Divorce of King Ammistamru II of Ugarit
1200	Incursions by the so-called "Sea Peoples" End of Hittite empire			
930 to 605	*Neo-Assyrian Period* Expansion of Assyria to Mediterranean and Egypt	Shamshi-Adad V (823–810) (wife Sammuramāt/ Semiramis)	Flourishing of art, especially reliefs in palaces	Inscriptions on buildings and reliefs, reports on military campaigns

Date	Political History		Civilization	Documents
		Adadnirari III (809–782) Sennacherib (704–681) (wife Naqi'a) Esarhaddon (680–669) Ashurbanipal (668–626) (wife Ashursharrat)	Monumental art of Tell Halaf (Guzana)	Famous library of Ashurbanipal at Nineveh, collection of Babylonian-Assyrian literature
625 to 539	*Neo-Babylonian Period* Again hegemony of Babylonia	Nebuchadnezzar II (604–562) Nabonidus (555–539) (mother Adad-guppi)	Built the "Hanging Gardens" for his wife Amytis, Babylon "metropolis of the world"	Numerous Babylonian economic documents
539		Conquest of Babylon by Cyrus II		
550	*Achaemenidian Period* Cyrus II (559–530) (founder of the Persian empire) Xerxes I (486–465) Darius III (335–330)		"Bank" of Murashu and Sons in Babylon	Commercial and other economic documents in Babylonian language
331	Alexander the Great defeats the Persians		Hellenistic and oriental art and civilizations further each other	
323	Death of Alexander the Great			
311 to 64	*Period of the Seleucid Empire* Founder Seleucus I, a general of Alexander		Foundation of Seleucia and Antioch	
approx. 250 B.C. to 224 A.D.	*Period of the Parthians* Phraates IV (37–2 B.C. (wife Musa) Phraates V and Thea Musa (2 B.C.–4 A.D.)		Prospering towns: Hatra, Palmyra, Dura-Europos, Edessa, centre of Syrian Christians	Aramaean inscriptions
approx. 224 to 651 A.D.	*Period of the Sassanids* Khosrau I (531–579 A.D.) Extermination of the followers of Mazdac Queen Buran (630–631)		Sassanid silver bowls and vases	Sassanid law code
660 A.D.	Conquest by Arabs		Islam spreads over Iran	

COMMENTS
ON ILLUSTRATIONS

ILLUSTRATIONS IN THE TEXT

PLATES

5 *Lyre Player and Female Singer*
Detail of so-called "Ur-standard," inlaid work of shells, lapis lazuli and red limestone, total height of standard: 20.3 cm., width: 48.3 cm., found in the royal cemetery of Ur, mid-3rd millennium B.C., London, British Museum, Inv. No. 121201

6 *Large Vase for Cultic Use, Decorated with Relief*
Detail from upper frieze, alabaster, total height of vessel: approx. 100 cm., Eanna sanctuary in Uruk, early 3rd millennium B.C., Baghdad, Iraq Museum

7 *Head of a Woman*
White marble, height: 20 cm., found in Uruk near the Eanna sanctuary, early 3rd millennium B.C., Baghdad, Iraq Museum

8 *Statuette of a Couple*
Gypsum, height: cm., from Nippur, mid-3rd millennium B.C., Baghdad, Iraq Museum

9 *Three Women*
Mosaic tablet of ivory, shells, slate, lapis lazuli and gold, from Mari, style of the Early Dynastic Period, Damascus, Museum (?)

10 *Head of Pin with two Small Nude Female Dancers*
Bronze, height: 18 cm., from Lagash, approx. mid-3rd millennium B.C., Paris, Louvre

11 *Woman's Jewellery*
Gold, lapis lazuli and cornelian, found in the royal cemetery of Ur, mid-3rd millennium B.C., London, British Museum

12 *Statuette of a Woman*
Gypsum, height: 26.2 cm., found in Ishtarat temple in Mari, mid-3rd millennium B.C., Damascus, Museum

13a) *Small Head of a Woman*
White limestone, hair made of bitumen, height: 12 cm., found in Tell Agrab, Diyala district, mid-3rd millennium B.C., Baghdad, Iraq Museum, Inv. No.27155

13b) *The Goddess Ninchursag*
Relief on fragment of stone vessel, height: 25 cm., probably from Lagash, approx. 2400 B.C., Berlin, Vorderasiatisches Museum, VA 7248

14a) and b) *Vase with Reliefs Representing the Goddess Narunde and the Priestess Kuri-Nahiti*
Silver, height: 19.3 cm., diagonal width of neck: 9 cm.; found in the plain of Persepolis, 23rd century B.C., Teheran, Museum of Antiquities

15 *Statuette of a Woman*
Silver and gold, height: 24.4 cm., from Hasanoglan near Ankara, approx. 2000 B.C., Ankara, Archaeological Museum

16 *Statuette of Praying Woman*
Alabaster, height: 22.8 cm., approx. mid-3rd millennium B.C., London, British Museum

17 *Small Head of a Woman*
Gypsum, height: 7.1 cm., from Ishthar temple in Ashur, approx. 2350 B.C., Berlin, Vorderasiatisches Museum, VA 6980

18a) *Erotic Scene*
Impression of cylinder seal, diameter: 2.2 cm., from Bahrein, early 2nd millennium B.C., Bahrein, National Museum

18b) *Impression of Cylinder Seal Representing an Erotic Scene*
Late 3rd millennium B.C., Paris, Louvre

19 *Impression of Cylinder Seal Representing a Harvest of Dates*
Height: 3 cm., Akkad period, approx. 2350 B.C., Den Haag, Koninklijk Kabinet van Munten, Penningen en Gesneden Stenen

20 *Statuette of a Woman*
Diorite, height: 17 cm., from Lagash, approx. 2050 B.C., Paris, Louvre, AO 295

21 *Representation of a Sacrifice*
Relief on limestone disc, diameter: 26.5 cm., from Ur, approx. 2300 B.C., Philadelphia, University Museum, Inv. No. CBS 1665

22 *Head of Goddess*
Terracotta, height: 5 cm., 22nd to 21st century B.C., Paris, Louvre

23 *Woman Seated on a Throne*
Relief on fragment of votive tablet, steatite, height: 14 cm., from Lagash, 22nd to 21st century B.C., Paris, Louvre

24 *Man and Woman Embracing*
Terracotta fragment from Nippur, approx. 2000 B.C., Chicago, University, Oriental Institute

25 *Bust of Woman*
Fragment of sculpture, limestone, height: 22 cm., allegedly from Umma, approx. 2000 B.C., Paris, Louvre

26 *Statuette of Priestess* (?)
Limestone, height (without head): 18.2 cm., approx. mid-3rd millennium B.C., Cologne, Collection Reg.-Baumeister Karl Band

27a) b) and c) *Couples of Lovers Lying on a Bed ("Sacred Marriage")*
Terracotta beds standing on four legs, early 2nd millennium B.C., Basle, Collection Frau Prof. Dr. Erlenmeyer

28 *Embracing Couple*
Terracotta relief, height: 11 cm., from Lagash, early 2nd millennium B.C., Paris, Louvre

29 *Goddess with Jewellery and Pleated Dress*
Fragment of relief in limestone, height: 13.5 cm., from the palace of Zimrilim in Mari, approx. 1700 B.C., Paris, Louvre, AO 19077

30 *Goddess with Wings and the Claws of Birds*
Terracotta, height: 50 cm., early 2nd millennium B.C., London, Collection Norman Colville

31 *Mother-Goddess Nintu*
Terracotta relief, height: 10 cm., early 2nd century B.C., Baghdad, Iraq Museum

32 *Goddess Dispensing Water*
Stone statue, height: 1.42 m., from the palace of Zim-rilim at Mari, approx. 1700 B.C., Aleppo, Museum

33 *Fish-Goddess*
Bronze statuette, height: 12 cm., from east of Susiana (?), 18th to 17th century B.C., London, British Museum, Inv. No. 132960

34 *Musicians*
Terracotta relief, height: 13.7 cm., first half of 2nd millennium B.C., Berlin, Vorderasiatisches Museum

35 *The Goddess Ishtar, Leading a King by the Hand*
Terracotta, height: 15 cm., approx. 1700 B.C., Jena, Hilprechtsammlung der Friedrich-Schiller-Universität, Inv. No. HS 44

36 *Pendant, Showing Astarte Nude, Standing on a Lion*
Gold, height: 6.5 cm., from Ugarit (Minet-el-Beida), 1450–1365 B.C., Paris, Louvre, AO 14714

37 *Nude Woman, Seated*
Probably the handle of a vessel, bronze, height: 6.7 cm., from Tell Asmar, Diyala District, 1st half of 2nd millennium B.C., Baghdad, Iraq Museum

38 *Erotic Scene*
Terracotta relief, height: 9.2 cm., 1st half of 2nd millennium B.C., London, British Museum

39a) *Nude Woman, Standing, Fertility Idol*
Terracotta, height: 16.3 cm., from Susa, mid-2nd millennium B.C., Paris, Louvre

39b) *Goddess, Uncovering her Privy Parts*
Impression of cylinder seal, hematite, height: 2.3 cm., diameter: 1.1 cm., old-Assyrian, approx. 1800 B.C., New York, Pierpont Morgan Library

40 *Representation of Man and Woman*
Relief on fragment of clay vessel, height of fragment: 36.5 cm., from Bitik near Ankara, period of Hittite Great Empire, approx. 1400 B.C., Ankara, Museum

41 *Statuette of Nude Goddess, Holding Child in her Arms*
Bronze, height: 18 cm., from Mitanni, mid-2nd millennium B.C., Berlin, Vorderasiatisches Museum

42 *Bead with Text and Scene Incised*
Light blue chalcedony, 4 by 3 by 1.8 cm., from Elam, 12th century B.C., London, British Museum, Inv. No. 113886 = 1919–7–12–12.635

43 *Backview of Female Statuette*
Ivory, height: approx. 23 cm., from Megiddo (Palestine), 13th century B.C., Chicago, University, Oriental Institute, No. A 22257

44a) *Spoon for Ointment with Figurative Handle*
Ivory, length: 19 cm., found in Ur, E-nun-mach Sanctuary, above room 15 of the Kassite building, London, British Museum

44b) *Comb Showing Women Carrying Offerings*
Incised ivory work, width: 6 cm., from grave 45 in Ashur, 14th century B.C., formerly in Berlin, Staatliche Museen

45 *Box (Toilet Requisite) Showing Female Musicians*
Ivory, height: 6.7 cm., found in south-eastern palace of Kalach-Nimrud, 9th to 8th century B.C., London, British Museum

46a) *Female Mask*
Grey-white frit with coloured inlay of bitumen, frit and glass, height: 11.8 cm., found in a sanctuary in Tell-al-Rimah, to the west of Mosul, mid-Assyrian period, 1380–1080 B.C.

46b) *Necklace of Larger and Smaller Beads*
Gold and semi-precious stones of various colours, first half of 1st millennium B.C., Berlin, Vorderasiatisches Museum

47 *Lid of Box Showing Goddess of Fertility Standing between two Goats*
Carved ivory with remains of painting, height: 15 cm., found in Minet-el-Beida, 14th to 13th century B.C., Paris, Louvre

48 *Detail of Statue of Queen Napir-asu of Elam*
Bronze, height: approx. 1.29 m., found in temple of Ninchursag in Susa, 13th century B.C., Paris, Louvre, SB 2731

49 *Noble Lady Spinning, with Female Servant*
Relief of dark bitumen, height: 10 cm., from Elam, approx. 1000 B.C. (?), Paris, Louvre

50 *Relief of the Goddess Ninchursag as Façade Ornament*
Burnt bricks, height of figure: 1.37 m., Susa, Inshushinak Temple, 12th century B.C., Paris, Louvre

51 *Boundary Stone of Melishipak, Introducing his Daughter to the Goddess Nanā*
Diorite, height: 90 cm., from Susa, Kassite period, 12th century B.C., Paris, Louvre

52 *The Goddess Kubaba*
Fragment of basalt relief, height: 82 cm., from Carchemish, early 1st millennium B.C., Ankara, Archaeological Museum, No. 103

53 *Tablet with Mid-Assyrian Law Code in Cuneiform Writing, so-called "Woman's Mirror", Tablet A*
Burnt clay, height: 32 cm., from Ashur, 12th century B.C., Berlin, Vorderasiatisches Museum

54 *Monumental Statue of Goddess (?)*
Basalt, height: 2.73 m., from Tell Halaf (Guzana), early 1st millennium B.C., Aleppo, Museum

55 *Goddess with Long Curled Locks, Seated*
Monumental sculpture in basalt, height: 1.92 m., from Tell Halaf (Guzana), early 1st millennium B.C., formerly Berlin, Tell-Halaf-Museum; cast in Aleppo, Museum

56 *Spinning Woman with Scribe*
Relief on Aramaic basalt stela, height: 1.05 m., from grave in Marash, 8th to 7th century B.C., Adana, Museum

57 *Young Scribe Standing on his Mother's Lap*
Relief on Aramaic basalt stela from grave, height: 80 cm., Marash, 8th to 7th century B.C., Paris, Louvre

58 *Pins for Garments*
Bronze, width: 3.1 to 11.9 cm., probably from Carchemish, 8th to 7th century B.C., Berlin, Vorderasiatisches Museum, VA 6999, VA 7000, VA 7002, VA 7004

59 *Couple Embracing*
Relief on Aramaic basalt stela, height: 100 cm., from grave in Marash, 8th to 7th century B.C., Adana, Museum

60 *and 61 a) Reliefs of Hierodules of the Goddess Astarte* (?)
Furniture ornaments, Phoenician ivory, height: 8.2 cm. and 6.8 cm., from Kalach-Nimrud, 8th century B.C., London, British Museum, Baghdad, Iraq Museum, Inv. No. 118859

61 b) *Woman Enthroned*
Ornament on a small box, Phoenician ivory, 8th century B.C., London, British Museum

62 *Esarhaddon and Naqi'a*
Relief on bronze tablet, height: 33 cm., from Ashur, 7th century B.C., Paris, Louvre

63 *Goddess Enthroned* (?)
Phoenician ivory, height: 11.7 cm., from Kalach-Nimrud, 8th century B.C., Baghdad, Iraq Museum

64 a) *Gold Pendant Showing Scene of Worship*
Replica, diameter: 4.6 cm., from Toprak-Kale at Van Lake, 8th to 7th century B.C., formerly Berlin, Staatliche Museen, VA 4634

64 b) *Breastplate with Adoration Scene Showing Priestess with Offering*
Silver, width: 6.5 cm., from Toprak-Kale at Van Lake, 8th to 7th century B.C., Berlin, Staatliche Museen, Vorderasiatisches Museum, VA 4635 b

65 *Pendant with Adoration Scene Showing Worship of Goddess Standing on a Lion*
Silver, diameter: 4.3 cm., from Sam'al, 8th to 7th century B.C., Berlin, Staatliche Museen, Vorderasiatisches Museum

66 *Man Hiding with his two Women in the Reeds*
Detail from an alabaster relief, height of total relief: approx. 1.45 m., found in room XXVIII of south-west palace of Sennacherib in Nineveh, approx. 700 B.C., London, British Museum, Inv. No. 124774

67 *Transport of Prisoners*
Relief on slab of limestone, height: 40 cm., width: 78 cm., from Kujundshik-Nineveh, 8th to 7th century B.C., London, Royal Geographical Society Museum

68 *Mirror with Figure of Nude Woman as Handle*
Bronze, height: approx. 27.3 cm., from Luristan, 8th to 7th century, Paris, Louvre AO 20181

69 *Statuette of Woman on Tripod-Candlestick*
Bronze, height: approx. 25 cm., Urartian, approx. 8th to 7th century B.C., Erlangen, Museum

70 a) *and b) Ashurbanipal with his Wife in the Vine Arbour*
Total view and detail of an alabaster relief, width: 1.39 m., from north palace of Ashurbanipal (668–630 B.C.) in Nineveh, London, British Museum, Inv. No. 124920

71 *Prisoners are Driven Away*
Detail of relief from south-west palace of Sennacherib in Nineveh, room XXXV, approx. 700 B.C., London, British Museum

72 *Head of a Woman, so-called "Mona Lisa"*
Furniture ornament, Phoenician ivory, height: approx. 16 cm., from north-west palace at Kalach-Nimrud, late 8th century B.C., Baghdad, Iraq Museum

73 *The Goddess Ishtar Standing on a Lion*
Impression of cylinder seal, green chalcedony, height: 4 cm., Assyrian, 750 to 650 B.C., London, British Museum, Inv. No. 89769

74 *Woman in Bathtub*
Clay, 8.3 by 10.8 cm., from the cemetery ez-Zib, Palestine, 9th to 6th century B.C., Jerusalem, Museum

75 a) *Pregnant Woman*
Terracotta, found in Phoenician cemetery in Akhziv, 6th to 4th century B.C., Jerusalem, Museum

75 b) *Woman with Child at her Breast*
Terracotta, height: 7 cm., from Uruk, first half of 1st millennium B.C., Berlin, Staatliche Museen, Vorderasiatisches Museum, W 6539, VA 11589

76 a) *b) and 77) Small Plaques with Erotic Scenes*
Lead, height: 7.2 cm.; 5.1 cm. and 6 cm., found in an Ishtar temple in Ashur, 8th to 7th century B.C., Berlin, Staatliche Museen, Vorderasiatisches Museum, VA Ass. 4244, VA Ass. 4245 and VA 5428

78 *Fragment of Sarcophagus Showing Riding Women*
Height: 1.24 m., length: 2.18 m., from Ergili-Daskyleion in Cilicia, Greco-Persian, early 5th century B.C., Istanbul, Archaeological Museum, No. 2358

79 *Fertility Goddess with Flute Player and Cithern Player*
Group of statues in limestone, height: 1.34 m., Phrygian, from Boghazköy, 2nd half of 6th century B.C., Ankara, Museum

80 *and 81 Tombstone Showing Ekphora (hearse) and Funeral Repast*
Total view and detail, white marble, total height: approx. 3 m., from Aksakal-Daskyleion in Cilicia, Greco-Persian, approx. 500 B.C., Istanbul, Archaeological Museum, No. 5763

82 *Jewellery*
Gold and silver, Parthian period, New Haven, Yale University, Art Gallery

83 *Statuette of Goddess of Love*
Alabaster partly decorated with bronze and gold, eyes and navel inlaid with garnets, height: 24 cm., found in Babylon, 3rd to 2nd century B.C., Paris, Louvre

84 *Statuette of Nude Woman, Standing*
Alabaster with headgear of bitumen, height: 19 cm., approx. 300 B.C. (?), Berlin, Staatliche Museen, Vorderasiatisches Museum, VA 281

85 *Sculpture of Reclining Nude Woman*
Alabaster, length: 13.4 cm., 2nd century B.C., Berlin, Staatliche Museen, Vorderasiatisches Museum, VA 2888

86 *Statuette of Nude Woman, Standing (without Head)*
Marble, height unknown, from Hatra, 2nd century A.D., Baghdad, Iraq Museum

87 *Coins: the Sassanid King Bahram I, with Wife and Crown-Prince, the Sassanid Queen Bura and the Parthian Queen Thea Musa*
Silver and gold, Parthian-Sassanid period, Berlin, Staatliche Museen, Münzkabinett

88 and 89 *Head of Young Girl*
Thin silver, height: 33.7 cm., Persian work, Parthian period, 1st century B.C. to 1st century A.D. (?), Washington, Freer Gallery of Art, Inv. No. 66.24

90 *Emblem Showing the Bust of Fertility Goddess in Relief*
Terracotta, from Susa, Greco-Parthian, 2nd to 1st century B.C., Paris, Louvre

91 *Statuette of Woman*
Lead, height: 13.7 cm., 1st century A.D., Stendal, Altmärkisches Museum, No. VIc-79

92 *Scene from Story of Moses*
Fresco from synagogue in Dura Europos, panel WC 4, scenes 1–2, Syrian-Roman, approx. 250 A.D., Damascus, Museum

93 *Funeral Repast*
Floor mosaic of rock grave, Edessa, 278 A.D., in situ

94 *Round Tablet Showing Bust of Moon Goddess*
Alabaster relief, diameter: 37 cm., from Temple II in Hatra, 1st to 2nd century A.D., Baghdad, Iraq Museum

95 *Parthian Standing in Front of a Goddess*
Terracotta relief made from mould bought at Aleppo, height: 12.5 cm., 2nd to 3rd century A.D., West Berlin, Staatliche Museen, Stiftung Preussischer Kulturbesitz, Islamisches Museum

96 *Tombstone Bust of Ammiat*
White limestone, height: approx. 52 cm., from Palmyra, 2nd to 4th century A.D., Paris, Louvre, Inv. No. AO 2196

97 *Tombstone Relief of Palmyrene Couple*
Limestone, height (?), Palmyra, 1st to 3rd century A.D., Damascus, Museum

98 *Tablet Showing Funeral Procession* (?)
Marble relief, height: approx. 1.30 m., from Baal's sanctuary in Palmyra, 1st century A.D., in situ

99 *Two Female Musicians on a Camel*
Terracotta, height: 22 cm., 2nd to 3rd century A.D. (?), Paris, Louvre

100 *Head of a Woman*
Height: 30 cm., from Palmyra, 2nd century A.D., Damascus (?)

101 *Relief of Goddess Ishtar*
From Palmyra, 1st to 3rd century A.D., Damascus, Museum

102 *Tombstone Bust of Palmyrene Woman*
Limestone, height: 58 cm., Palmyra, 2nd to 3rd century A.D., Amherst, The Classical Collection of Amherst College

103 *Tombstone Relief of Palmyrene Woman with Female Servant*
2nd to 3rd century A.D., Damascus, Museum

104 *Statue of Ubal, Daughter of Jabal*
Limestone, height: 1.70 m., from temple IV in Hatra, 2nd century A.D., Baghdad, Iraq Museum

105 *Impression of Seal with Incised Head of a Woman*
Transparent stone, height: ? cm., Sassanid, 3rd century A.D., Leningrad, Hermitage

106 *Mosaic with Representation of Female Harpist*
Floor mosaic of the Liwan (room open on one side), 85 by 64 cm., from Bishapur, Iranian-Roman, second half of 3rd century A.D., Paris, Louvre

107 *Rhyton (Drinking Vessel) in the Shape of a Woman's and a Bull's Head*
Silver, partly gilded, height: approx. 19 cm., found in Dailaman district of Iran, Sassanid, 4th to 6th century A.D., Cleveland, The Cleveland Museum of Art

108 *Sculpture of Young Woman (Moon Goddess)*
Limestone, height: 72 cm., building sculpture of Hatra, 1st to 2nd century A.D., Berlin, Staatliche Museen, Stiftung Preussischer Kulturbesitz

109 *Vase Showing Face of Woman*
Silver, Sassanid, 3rd to 5th century A.D., Leningrad, Hermitage

110 *Bowl Decorated with Nude Figure of Goddess Anahita*
Silver, partly gilded, diameter: approx. 21 cm., Sassanid, early 4th century A.D., Cleveland, The Cleveland Museum of Art, Purchased from the John L. Severance Fund, 62.295

111 *Vase with Relief Ornaments*
Silver, partly gilded, height: 18 cm., from the Dailaman district, Iran, Sassanid, 4th to 6th century A.D., Paris, Louvre, Inv. No. MAO 424

112 *Bowl Showing Royal Banquet*
Silver, diameter: approx. 23 cm., Sassanid, 6th to 7th century A.D., Baltimore, Maryland, The Walters Art Gallery

BIBLIOGRAPHY

1 Al-Zeebari, A.: *Altbabylonische Briefe des Iraq-Museums*, Cologne 1964

2 Andrae, W.: *Die jüngeren Ischtar Tempel in Assur*, WVDOG 58, 1935

3 Artzi, P.; Malamat, A.: *The Correspondence of Šibtu, Queen of Mari* in ARM X, Orientalia NS 40, 1971, 75–89

4 Avesta: *Die Heiligen Bücher der Parsen*, translated by Fritz Wolff, Berlin and Leipzig 1924

5 Bartholomae, Chr.: *Die Frau im sasanidischen Recht, Kultur und Sprache 5*, Heidelberg 1924

6 Bengtson, H.: *Alexander und die Eroberung des Perserreiches.* In: Fischer Weltgeschichte 5, Frankfort/M and Hamburg 1971

7 Biggs, R. D.: ŠÀ.ZI.GA. *Ancient Mesopotamian Potency Incantations* (= Texts from Cuneiform Sources, Vol. 2), New York 1967

8 Böhl, F. M. Th.: *Die Tochter des Königs Nabonid.* In: Symbolae ad Iura Orientis Antiqui Pertinentes Paulo Koschaker Dedicatae, Leyden 1939, 151–178

9 Brentjes, B.: *Die iranische Welt vor Mohammed*, Leipzig 1967

10 Burrows, M.: *The Basis of Israelite Marriage.* American Oriental Series 15, New Haven 1938

11 Deimel, P. A.: *Sumerische Tempelwirtschaft zur Zeit Urukaginas und seiner Vorgänger.* Analecta Orientalia 2, Rome 1931

12 Descamps, P.: *La Situation de la Femme chez les Anciens Sémites.* Revue Internationale de Sociologie, 37th year, Nos. I–II, 1929

13 Donner, H.: *Art und Herkunft des Amtes der Königinmutter im Alten Testament.* In: Festschrift Johannes Friedrich zum 65. Geburtstag, Heidelberg 1959, 105–145

14 Ebeling, E.: *Liebeszauber im Alten Orient.* MAOG 1, H. 1, Leipzig 1925

15 Ebeling, E.: *Aus dem Tagewerk eines assyrischen Zauberpriesters.* MAOG 5, H. 3, Leipzig 1931

16 Ebeling, E.: *Neubabylonische Briefe.* Abhandlungen Bayrische Akademie der Wissenschaften, philosophisch-historische Klasse, NF 30, Munich 1949, 110

17 Ebeling, E.: *Stiftungen und Vorschriften für assyrische Tempel.* Schriften der Deutschen Akademie der Wissenschaften zu Berlin. Institut für Orientforschung, Veröffentlichung Nr. 23, Berlin 1954

18 Ebeling, E.: In: Reallexikon der Assyriologie und vorderasiatischen Archäologie, vol. 3, 1971, *Familie*, p. 12

19 Edzard, D. O.: *Sumerische Rechtsurkunden des III. Jahrtausends aus der Zeit vor der III. Dynastie von Ur.* Abhandlungen der Bayrischen Akademie der Wissenschaften, philosophisch-historische Klasse, NF 67, Munich 1968

20 Eydoux, H.-P.: *Les grandes Dames de l'Archéologie*, Paris 1964

ABBREVIATIONS

AASOR	Annual of the American Schools of Oriental Research
BASOR	Bulletin of the American Schools of Oriental Research
CE	Codex Eshnunna
CH	Codex Hammurabi
CLI	Codex Lipit-Ishtar
Heth	Hethitische Rechtssammlung
JAOS	Journal of the American Oriental Society
JNES	Journal of Near Eastern Studies
MAOG	Mitteilungen der Altorientalischen Gesellschaft
MAss	Mittelassyrisches Rechtsbuch ("Woman's Mirror")
MJ	Museum Journal
MVAeG	Mitteilungen der Vorderasiatisch-Aegyptischen Gesellschaft
WVDOG	Wissenschaftliche Veröffentlichungen der Deutschen Orientgesellschaft
ZA NF	Zeitschrift für Assyriologie, Neue Folge

21 Falkenstein, A.: *Die neusumerischen Gerichtsurkunden.* Abhandlungen der Bayrischen Akademie der Wissenschaften, philosophisch-historische Klasse, NF 39, Munich 1956–1957

22 Falkenstein, A.: *akiti-Fest und akiti-Festhaus.* In: Festschrift Johannes Friedrich zum 65. Geburtstag, Heidelberg 1959, 147–182

23 Finkelstein, J. J.: *Sex Offences in Sumerian Laws,* JAOS 86, 1966, 355–372

24 Fisher, L. R.; Knutson, F. B.: *An Enthronement Ritual at Ugarit.* JNES 28, 1969, 157–167

25 Frankena, R.: *Briefe aus dem British Museum,* Leyden 1966

26 Frankena, R.: *Briefe aus der Leidener Sammlung,* Leyden 1968

27 Friedrich, J.: *Churritische Märchen und Sagen in hethitischer Sprache.* ZA NF 15, 1949, 213–255

28 Gadd, C. J.: *The Harran Inscriptions of Nabonidus.* Anatolian Studies 8, 1958, 35–92

29 Goetze, A.: *Kleinasien* (= Handbuch der Altertumswissenschaft), Munich 1957

30 Gordon, C. H.: *Fifteen Nuzi Tablets relating to Women.* Le Muséon 48, 1935, 113–132

31 Gordon, C. H.: *The Status of Woman Reflected in the Nuzi Tablets.* ZA NF 9, 1936, 146–169

32 Gordon, C. H.: *A New Akkadian Parallel to Deuteronomy,* 25, 11–12, Journal of the Palestine Oriental Society 15, 1935, 29–34

33 Gordon, E. I.: *Sumerian Proverbs,* Philadelphia 1959

34 Greengus, S.: *Old Babylonian Marriage Ceremonies and Rites.* Journal of Cuneiform Studies 20, 1966, 55–72

35 Greengus, S.: *The Old Babylonian Marriage Contract.* JAOS 89, 1969, 505–532

36 Grimal, P. (ed.): *Histoire Mondiale de la Femme.* Book Three: *La Femme dans l'Asie Occidentale Ancienne: Mésopotamie et Israel* by Jean Bottéro. *Chez les Hittites* by Jenny Danmanville. Paris 1965

37 Haase, R.: *Die keilschriftlichen Rechtssammlungen in deutscher Übersetzung,* Wiesbaden 1963

38 Hallo, W. W.: *The Slandered Bride.* In: Studies presented to A. Leo Oppenheim, Chicago 1964, 95–105

39 Hamdun, S.: *Die Frau in der irakischen Gesellschaft und ihre Rolle in der nationalen Befreiungsbewegung (1945–1963).* University thesis, Berlin 1971

40 Harris, R.: *The Organization and Administration of the Cloister in Ancient Babylonia.* Journal of Economic and Social History of the Orient 6, 1963, 121–157

41 Harris, R.: *The Nadītu Woman.* In: Studies presented to A. Leo Oppenheim, Chicago 1964, 106–135

42 Harris, R.: *Notes on the Babylonian Cloister and Hearth.* Orientalia NS 38, 1969, 133 seq.

43 Hecker, K.: *Die Keilschrifttexte der Universitätsbibliothek Gießen* (= Berichte und Arbeiten aus der Universitätsbibliothek Gießen. 9), Giessen 1966

44 Helck, W.: *Betrachtungen zur großen Göttin und den ihr verbundenen Gottheiten* (= Religion und Kultur der Alten Mittelmeerwelt in Parallelforschungen. 2), Munich and Vienna 1971

45 Hinz, W.: *Das Reich Elam,* Stuttgart 1964

46 Hinz, W.: *Elams Vertrag mit Narām-Sin von Akkade.* ZA NF 24, 1967, 86

47 Hinz, W.: *Eine neugefundene altelamische Silbervase* (= Altiranische Funde und Forschungen), 1969, 11–27

48 Jeremias, A.: *Handbuch der altorientalischen Geisteskultur,* Berlin and Leipzig 1929

49 Klíma, J.: *Die Stellung der ugaritischen Frau.* Archiv Orientální 25, 1957, 313–332

50 Klíma, J.: *Donationes mortis causa nach den akkadischen Urkunden aus Susa.* In: Festschrift Johannes Friedrich zum 65. Geburtstag, Heidelberg 1959, 229–259

51 Klíma, J.: *Gesellschaft und Kultur des alten Mesopotamien,* Prague 1964

52 Klíma, O.: *Zur Problematik der Ehe-Institution im alten Iran.* Archiv Orientální 34, 1966, 554–569

53 König, F. W.: *Mutterrecht und Thronfolge im alten Elam.* In: Festschrift der Nationalbibliothek in Wien, herausgegeben zur Feier des 200jährigen Bestehens des Gebäudes, Vienna 1926

54 Kohler, J.; Ungnad, A.: *Hammurabi's Gesetz.* III., IV., Leipzig 1909/1910

55 Kohler, J.; Ungnad, A.: *Assyrische Rechtsurkunden,* Leipzig 1913

56 Korošec, V.: *Über die neuesten sumerischen Gesetzesfragmente aus Ur.* Bibliotheca Orientalis 25, 1968, 288

57 Kramer, S. N.: *Sumerian Literary Texts from Nippur in the Museum of the Ancient Orient at Istanbul,* AASOR 23, 1944, No. 129

58 Kramer, S. N.: *From the Tablets of Sumer,* Indian Hills, Colorado, 1956

59 Kramer, S. N.: *Sumerische literarische Texte aus Nippur* (= Texte und Materialien der Frau Prof. Hilprecht-Sammlung Vorderasiatischer Altertümer im Eigentum der Friedrich Schiller Universität Jena, NF 3), Berlin 1961

60 Kramer, S. N.: *The Sumerians. Their History, Culture and Character,* Chicago 1963

61 Kramer, S. N.: *Cuneiform Studies and the History of Literature: the Sumerian Sacred Marriage Texts.* Proceedings of the American Philosophical Society 107, 1963, 485–527

62 Kramer, S. N.: *Sumerian Sacred Marriage Songs and the Biblical "Song of Songs".* Mitteilungen des Instituts für Orientforschung 15, Berlin 1969, 262–274

63 Kraus, F. R.: *Briefe aus dem British Museum,* Leyden 1964

64 Kraus, F. R.: *Briefe aus dem Archive des Šamaš-ḫazir in Paris und Oxford,* Leyden 1968

65 Kraus, P.: *Altbabylonische Briefe aus der Vorderasiatischen Abteilung der Preußischen Staatsmuseen zu Berlin.* II. MVAeG 36, 1932

66 Labat, R.: *Assyrien und seine Nachbarländer*. In: Fischer Weltgeschichte 4, Frankfort/Main and Hamburg 1967, 42

67 Lambert, W. G.: *Morals in Ancient Mesopotamia*. Jaarbericht 15. Ex Oriente Lux, 1957–1958, 184–196

68 Lambert, W. G.: *Babylonian Wisdom Literature*, Oxford 1960

69 Lambert, W. G.: *Middle Assyrian Medical Text*, Iraq 31, 1969

70 Landsberger, B.: *Jungfräulichkeit: Ein Beitrag zum Thema "Beilager und Eheschließung"*. In: Symbolae Iuridicae et Historicae Martino David Dedicatae, Leyden 1968, 41–105

71 Leemans, W. F.: *The Old Babylonian Merchant, his Business and his Social Position* (= Studia et Documenta ad Iura Orientis Antiqui Pertinentia. 3), Leyden 1950

72 Leemans, W. F.: *Old Babylonian Letters and Economic History*, Leyden 1968

73 Lehmann-Haupt, C. F.: *Die historische Semiramis und ihre Zeit*, Tübingen 1910

74 Malamat, A.: *Syrien-Palästina in der zweiten Hälfte des 2. Jahrtausends*. In: Fischer Weltgeschichte 3, Frankfort/Main and Hamburg 1966, 188

75 Marx, V.: *Die Stellung der Frau in Babylonien gemäß den Kontrakten aus der Zeit von Nebukadnezar bis Darius (604–485)*. Beiträge zur Assyriologie 4, 1902, 1–77

76 Matouš, L.: *Some Remarks to the Economical Sources from Larsa*, Archiv Orientální 23, 1955, 465–474

77 Meißner, B.: *Babylonien und Assyrien* I/II, Heidelberg 1920/1925

78 Meißner, B.: *Der Kuß im Alten Orient*. Sitzungsberichte der Preußischen Akademie der Wissenschaften, philosophisch-historische Klasse, 28, 1934

79 Mellaart, J.: *Čatal Hüyük–A Neolithic Town in Anatolia*, London 1967

80 Mendelsohn, I.: *The Conditional Sale into Slavery of Freeborn Daughters in Nuzi and the Law of Exodus 21: 7–11*. JAOS 55, 1935, 190–195

81 Mendelsohn, I.: *Slavery in the Ancient Near East*, New York 1949

82 Meuleau, M.: *Mesopotamien in der Perserzeit*. In: Fischer Weltgeschichte 5, Frankfort/Main and Hamburg 1971

83 Moortgat, A.: *Tammuz*, Berlin 1949

84 Moortgat, A.: *Geschichte Vorderasiens bis zum Hellenismus* (= Weltgeschichte in Einzeldarstellungen), Munich 1950

85 Moran, W. L.: *The Scandal of the "Great Sin" at Ugarit*. JNES 18, 1959, 280 seq.

86 Muntingh, L. M.: *The Social and Legal Status of a Free Ugaritic Female*. JNES 26, 1967, 102–112

87 Nöldeke, Th.: *Geschichte der Perser und Araber zur Zeit der Sasaniden. Aus der arabischen Chronik des Tabari*, Leyden 1879

88 Nougayrol, J.: *Textes Accadiens des Archives Sud. Le Palais Royal d'Ugarit*, publié sous la Direction de Claude F.-A. Schaeffer. IV, Paris 1956

89 Oppenheim, L.: *Letters from Mesopotamia*, Chicago and London 1967

90 Otten, H.: *Hethiter, Hurriter und Mitanni*. In: Fischer Weltgeschichte 3, Frankfort/Main and Hamburg 1966

91 Pfeiffer, R. H.; Speiser, E. A.: *One Hundred New Selected Nuzi Texts*. AASOR 16, 1936

92 Renger, J.: *Untersuchungen zum Priestertum in der altbabylonischen Zeit*. ZA NF 24, 1967, 110–188

93 Röllig, W.: *Erwägungen zu neuen Stelen Nabonids*. ZA NF 22, 1964, 218–260

94 Römer, W. H. Ph.: *Einige Beobachtungen zur Göttin Nini(n)sina auf Grund von Quellen der Ur-III-Zeit und der altbabylonischen Periode*. In: lišān mithurti. Festschrift Wolfram Freiherr von Soden, Neukirchen-Vluyn 1969, 279–305

95 Sachau, E.: *Von den rechtlichen Verhältnissen der Christen im Sasanidenreich*. Mitteilungen des Seminars für Orientalische Sprachen an der Kgl. Friedrich-Wilhelms-Universität zu Berlin, year 10, Berlin 1907, 69–95

96 Schmökel, H.: *Das Gilgamesch-Epos*, Stuttgart, Berlin, Cologne, Mainz 1966

97 Schuler, E. von: *Hethitische Dienstanweisungen für höhere Hof- und Staatsbeamte*. Archiv für Orientforschung, Beiheft 10, Graz 1957

98 San Nicolò, M.; Petschow, H.: *Babylonische Rechtsurkunden aus dem 6. Jahrhundert v. Chr.* Abhandlungen der Bayrischen Akademie der Wissenschaften, philosophisch-historische Klasse, NF 51, Munich 1960

99 Sasson, J. N.: *Instances of Mobility among Mari Artisans*. BASOR 190, 1968, 46–54

100 Selms, A. van: *Marriage and Family Life in Ugarit Literature* (= Pretoria Oriental Series. 1), London 1954

101 Skaist, A.: *The Authority of the Brother at Arrapha and Nuz (Nuzi)*. JAOS 89, 1969, 10–17

102 Soden, W. von: *Eine altbabylonische Beschwörung gegen die Dämonin Lamaštum*. Orientalia NS 23, 1954, 339

103 Soden, W. von: *Die Hebamme in Babylon und Assyrien*. Archiv für Orientforschung 18, 1957–1958, 119–121

104 Speiser, E. A.: *New Kirkuk Documents Relating to Family Laws*. AASOR 10, 1928–1929, 1–73

105 Speiser, E. A.: *A Significant New Will from Nuzi*. Journal of Cuneiform Studies 17, 1963

106 Spycket, A.: *La Coiffure Féminine en Mésopotamie des Origines à la 1re Dynastie de Babylon*. Revue d'Assyriologie et d'Archéologie orientale 48/49, 1954/1955, 169–177, 113–128 resp.

107 Steele, F. R.: *Nuzi Real Estate Transactions*. American Oriental Series 25, 1943

108 Strommenger, E.: *Eine altmesopotamische Würdenträger-innenstatuette der Farah/Ur I-Zeit* (= Festschrift zum Hundertjährigen Bestehen der Berliner Gesellschaft für Anthropologie, Ethnologie und Urgeschichte. II), Berlin 1970, 232–235

109 Sturtevant, E. H.: *A Hittite Text on the Duties of Priests and Temple Servants.* JAOS 54, 1934

110 Van Praag, A.: *Droit Matrimonial Assyro-Bablonien*, Amsterdam 1945

111 Waschow, H.: *Babylonische Briefe aus der Kassitenzeit.* MAOG 10, No. 1, 1936

112 Weidner, E.: *Hof- und Harems-Erlasse assyrischer Könige aus dem 2. Jahrtausend v. Chr.* Archiv für Orientforschung 17, 1954–1956, 257–293

113 Weidner, E.: *Eine Erbteilung in mittelassyrischer Zeit.* Archiv für Orientforschung 20, 1963, 123

114 Werner, R.: *Die hethitischen Gerichtsprotokolle.* Wiesbaden 1967

115 Wilcke, C.: *Die akkadischen Glossen in TMH NF 3, Nr. 25 und eine neue Interpretation des Textes.* Archiv für Orientforschung 23, 1970, 84–87

116 Yaron, R.: *A Royal Divorce at Ugarit.* Orientalia NS 32, 1963, 21–31

SOURCES OF ILLUSTRATIONS

The authors and publishers wish to thank the following persons, museums and institutions who made items available for reproduction in this book:

Basel, Collection Erlenmeyer 27a, b, c
The Hague, Koniklijk Kabinet van Munten, Pennigen en Gesneden Stenen 19
London, D.M.E. Mallowan 63
Paris, C.F.A. Schaeffer 36, 47
Paris, André Parrot 9
Philadelphia, University Museum 2, 21

Aarhus, Geoffrey Bibby 18a
Aleppo, National Museum 54, 55
Amherst, The Classical Collection of Amherst College 102
Baghdad, Iraq-Museum, Directorate General of Antiquities 7, 31, 61b, 94, 104
Baltimore, The Walthers Art Gallery 112
Basel, D. Widmer 27a, b, c
Berlin, Staatliche Museen 13b, 17, 34, 41, 44b, 46b, 53, 58, 64a, b, 65, 75b, 76a, b, 77, 84, 85, 87
Berlin (West), Staatliche Museen, Stiftung Preussischer Kulturbesitz 95, 108
Berlin, Burchard Brentjes 71
Chicago, University of Chicago, Oriental Institute 24, 43
Cleveland, The Cleveland Museum of Art 107, 110
Cologne, Regierungs-Baumeister Karl Band 26
Cologne, M. DuMont Schauberg Publishers 21
Damascus, National Museum 97, 101, 103
Erlangen, Kunstsammlung der Friedrich-Alexander-Universität 69

Florence, SCALA, Istituto Fotografico Editoriale 8, 37, 86
Göttingen, Walter Hinz 14
Halle, Ottfried Birnbaum 19
Istanbul-Taksim, German Archeological Institute, Department Istanbul, Photos: W. Schiele 78, 79, 80, 81
Jena, University Photo Department 35
Jerusalem, Ministry of Education and Culture, The Israel Department of Antiquities and Museums 74, 75a
Leipzig, Koehler & Amelang 2
Leningrad, Hermitage 105, 109
London, British Museum, Department of Photographic Service 5, 11, 33, 38, 42, 44a, 61a, 66b, 70a, b, 73
London, Collins Publishers 63
London, Norman Colville 30
London, David Oates 46a
London, James Mellaart 1, 4
London, Royal Geographical Society 67
London, J. B. Segal 93
Munich, Hirmer-Fotoarchiv 3, 6, 12, 13a, 15, 16, 22, 29, 32, 40, 45, 48, 52, 56, 59, 60, 66a, 72
New Haven, Yale University Art Gallery 82, 92
New York, Pierpont Morgan Library 39b
Paris, Musée du Louvre, Service de Documentation Photographique de la Réunion des Musées Nationaux 18b, 20, 23, 25, 28, 39a, 49, 50, 51, 57, 62, 90, 99
Paris, Maurice Chuzeville 10, 36, 47, 68, 83, 96, 106, 111
Stendal, O. Palm 91
Warsaw, Andrzej 98
Warsaw, Michael Gawlikowski 100
Washington, Smithsonian Institution, Freer Gallery of Art 88, 89

PLATES

Mother goddess giving birth (approx. 5800 B.C.). She symbolizes the religious beliefs in prehistoric times. As the mistress of all animals she sits on a throne supported by animals while giving birth to a child, *to "life." Other images represent her as the manifestation of death, as she was everything at once: mother goddess, death goddess, mistress of the animals, and thus the most sacred figure of these epochs.*

This fertility idol of the 3rd millennium B.C. shows that preference was given at that time to curved and luxuriant bodily shapes which symbolized plenty and fertility; yet the charms of a slim waist and of rich jewellery, too, were not ignored.

This terracotta statuette of the Halaf period (4th millennium B.C.) stresses exuberant femininity and fecundity of women, typical for that civilization. The red paint might indicate tattooing or painting of the body.

Jewellery from Catalhuyuk (approx. 5800 B.C.). Already at that time multi-coloured stones were cut, polished and threaded in wearisome labour to form bright necklaces and bracelets. Technically this deserves great admiration; the excavators reported that their own needles were not thin enough to pass through the ancient hollows.

This detail from the so-called "Ur-standard" shows that music was not absent from festivities, male and female singers accompanied their recitals and songs by playing on the lyre. Precious lyres have been found near the skeletons of women who were buried together with their kings in the royal graves of Ur.

This picture from the famous "Uruk vase" (early 3rd millennium B.C.) witnesses to the high position woman occupied in the cult. Standing as representative of the goddess in front of the temple, she accepted tribute from the people. Like a ruler, she is repeatedly shown as a dominating personality in contemporary works of art.

The woman's head from Uruk is one of the most famous relics of the Ancient East. The delicately moulded features seem to be those of a priestess of the mother goddess Innin. Unfortunately, it was found impossible to reconstruct her coiffure. The thin face with large nose and large dark eyes and eyebrows no doubt corresponds to the contemporary ideal of beauty.

Couples in loving embrace were often represented in the Ancient East. The present examples date from the Early Dynastic period (mid-3rd millennium).

Three women are occupied working, though the kind of work cannot be identified (perhaps spinning?). This inlaid work from Mari is interesting as a small fashion catalogue: on the head, the women wear caps or artistically pleated scarves; the dresses are held together on the chest with pins, to which pendants are fastened with cords.

9

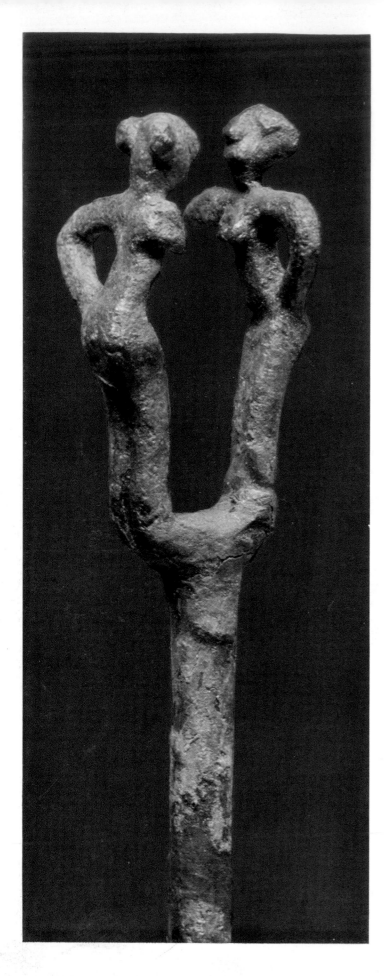

Two small nude female dancers form the top of a bronze pin (approx. mid-3rd millennium). Dancing played an important role in the ancient civilizations and occupied a substantial place in the cult.

Precious jewellery like this was worn by the women, who were buried in the royal graves at Ur together with their rulers, so as to be at their disposal also in the beyond (mid-3rd millennium B.C.). They probably wore garments of thin red wool, of which very small remains have been found.

Statuette of an enthroned woman from Mari. Fringed garments like hers are typical of the Early Dynastic period; they probably replaced the original garments made of fur and were made of a kind of rough fabric like a bath towel, arranged in several flounces. The "polos" (a high headdress, tapering off at the top and fastened at the bottom with a broad ribbon) is characteristic of the women (goddesses?) of Mari, while the hair puffed up over the ears was popular also in other areas.

This small sculpture of a head shows the carefully arranged headdress of a lady of the Early Dynastic period. The finely pleated "turban" left the black hair uncovered only on the forehead and over the ears; the artist used inlaid black bitumen to represent the hair.

The figure on this fragment of a vase for ritual use from approximately 2400 B.C., probably represents the Sumeric goddess Ninchursag. Gods and goddesses can usually be recognized by their "horn-crown." The life-giving forces of the goddess are here symbolized by the twigs sprouting out of her horn-crown, the ears of corn over her shoulders and the cluster of dates, which she holds in her hand.

"Help, Mistress, help! I am the giver of drink-offerings for the goddess, I Kuri-Nahiti. Appear, divine mistress, bringing reward and blessing." This is the inscription on this silver vase from Elam (23rd century B.C.). The standing goddess invoked by the crouching priestess is Narunde.

Fertility idols are to be found in large numbers in old-oriental art; their style changed in the course of time as tastes altered. It seems that at approximately 2000 B.C. a slim maidenly type was preferred in Asia Minor, where this valuable idol was found.

15

The young praying woman, with her hands devoutly crossed in front, has attractive curls at her ears and her forehead. She has plenty of hair, combed upwards and puffed out. Her fringed coat is passed under the right arm and covers her left shoulder.

The little head from Ashur, from approximately 2350 B.C. seems to be the portrait of a pretty young woman. Her hair is held together by a scarf and turned in at the neck. Unfortunately, the inlaid works for the eyes and eye-brows are damaged.

17

This seal and its impression show a woman in an unequivocal attitude. It is not clear whether this represents a mythological scene or is a "love magic" with a magician priest.

19

Women harvesting dates. They worked frequently in this important branch of agriculture in the Ancient Orient, picking fruit. Supplying a basic food, the date tree was the cultic "lifetree."

This statuette of the 21st century B.C. is proof that fashion and taste became highly refined in the course of time. The hair was carefully waved and covered with a bonnet of fine cloth. Several rings of gold around the neck formed part of the noble lady's attire; her garment was decorated with embroidered ornaments. The colours purple and blue were particularly valued.

Representation of a sacrifice. Encheduanna, the famous daughter of the famous Sargon of Akkad (approximately 2300 B.C.), is shown performing a ritual act. As en-priestess she wore a special costume: a cap with rolled-up edge and a frilled garment. According to the texts, other items forming part of this priestly attire were a piece of jewellery called mush-mush, and a mace.

Head of a goddess with a three-tier "horn-crown," her insignia as a
deity.

An inscription dedicates this votive tablet to the goddess Ninsun. The
whole appearance of this woman, seated on a throne, with all the
fashionable details certainly show her to have been the ideal of the
contemporary woman.

A couple in a loving embrace is to be seen on this terracotta fragment from approximately 2000 B.C. Especially charming is the artistically pinned up hair of the woman.

This woman of the Neo-Sumerian period of approximately 2000 B.C. wears a virtually outmoded garment. At this period recourse was taken consciously — in particular in religious observances — to earlier epochs, and this is shown also in clothes. Thus, the woman portrayed here, who no doubt belonged to the staff of the temple, let herself be represented dressed in one of the fringed garments of earlier times.

This interesting and so far unique statuette (approximately mid-3rd millennium) probably represents a priestess, the "bride" of the "Sacred Marriage." On a chain slung round her neck she wears a small but precious "bed" on which a nude couple is to be seen performing the blessed ritual meant to ensure fertility.

"... I want to make love to you in the moonlight! On the clean bed filled with voluptuousness, I will loosen your combs ..." (115)

This terracotta relief (early 2nd millennium B.C.) shows a warm human relationship between man and wife. According to the contemporary fashion the woman wears a dress wrapped around her body, at the hems it is decorated with fringes; nor are the typical rings around the neck missing. A thick knot of hair like hers is often enclosed in a fine net or ribbon to keep it tidy.

Goddess inhaling the scent of a flower (18th century B.C.). According to the beliefs of that time gods and goddesses felt like men, and thus a goddess evidently did not disdain to seek comfort in the scent of a flower, a charming theme shown by the artist.

This winged goddess, with the claws of birds and accompanied by owls and lions, may well have frightened men of the early 2nd millennium B.C., but the masterly artist of the Ancient East also has represented here in the most perfect manner—long before Greek art—the sensuous and aesthetic charm of the nude female body.

The goddess Nintu. In the course of the centuries the mother goddess has been invoked under many different names: Innin, Ishtar, Baba, Ninchursag, Ninmach and many more, thus also as Nintu, who is represented in this relief as helping mothers and women in travail. She has been depicted holding children to her breast (?) or on her back; the ribbon-like designs at both her sides on this relief symbolize the life-giving womb.

Goddess dispensing water. In the countries of the East, many of which are dependent on artificial irrigation, water plays an essential role and was worshipped in the shape of a goddess. Inside this large almost life-size statue was a canal through which water could be poured into a vessel, so that the goddess could in fact "dispense" water to the devout believers.

The fish-goddess, too, testifies to the importance of water — and thereby of the fish, one of the main foodstuffs. Into the goddess's open hands the worshippers no doubt put small offerings.

A woman playing the lyre and a dancer with a tambourine exhibit their art. In the Ancient East gay and exuberant joie de vivre was always expressed by dance and play, which also occupied a permanent place in the cult.

A terracotta relief from the Old-Babylonian period shows the goddess Ishtar together with a king (Hammurabi?). The kings liked to be represented together with "their" deity and thereby to prove that their reign was "willed by god."

A golden pendant, found in the harbour district of Ugarit, where the goddess of love was bound to be very popular. She appears again and again in an ever new shape. Here it probably is Astarte, the Mesopotamian "Ishtar," who dominates animals, and, herself nude, stands on a lion. Even King Solomon was said to have worshipped her and to have dedicated a temple to her.

Most likely this small nude woman's figure formed the handle of a bronze vessel. Worth noting is the vivacity of the representation, unconventional at that period.

This female idol of clay from the mid-2nd millennium B.C. symbolizes fertility and sensual lust by showing bulging and exuberant forms.

A goddess, gathering up her dress (approx. 1800 B.C.). There are frequent examples of women, uncovering their privy parts, either as an insult (especially when prisoners) or to avert misfortune, to drive away the enemy, etc. But on this seal it is certainly meant to enhance fertility and the enjoyment of love.

This fragment of a Hittite clay vessel with relief decorations (approximately 1400 B.C.) shows a man and a woman seated in an open door or a window. The man offers a drinking bowl to the woman; she wears the wrap usual at that time, which covers a large part of her head and her body.

This bronze statuette from the mid-2nd millennium B.C. stresses the motherly aspect of the nude goddess, who, like the Mesopotamian Ishtar, has chosen the lion as her animal companion.

There is an inscription on this bead (left, full size). The father arranged the moment of the presentation to be retained in this picture.

"I, Shilhak-Inshushinak,
Who enlarged the empire,
Have brought this jasper bead
From the land of Puralish.
I let it be worked carefully
And had it mounted and
Then gave it to Bar-Uli,
My beloved daughter." (45)

This attractive ivory figure is that of a woman, wearing a crown, from under this, her hair, hanging down over her body, is artistically arranged in a broad plait. The front of the figure is badly damaged.

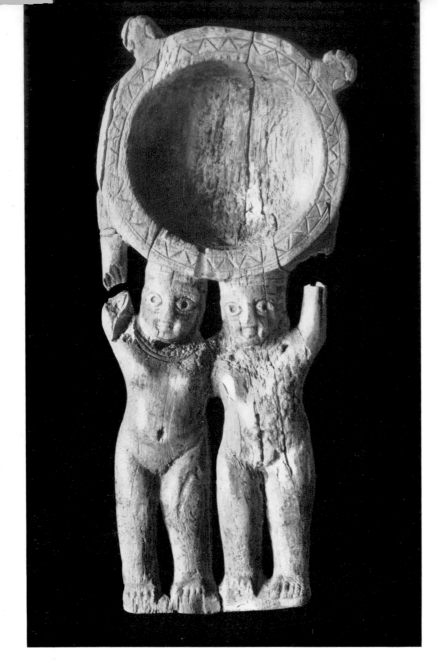

The small figures of two nude young maidens form the handle of an ivory spoon to be used for ointments. In the East, the use of ointments was deemed as essential to life as eating or drinking; even the images of the gods were treated with it.

This ivory comb from Ashur (14th century B.C.) is decorated with an incised drawing: women in richly embroidered garments bring offerings to a goddess who is shown on the reverse side of the comb. The women are accompanied by a female harpist or lyre player (left).

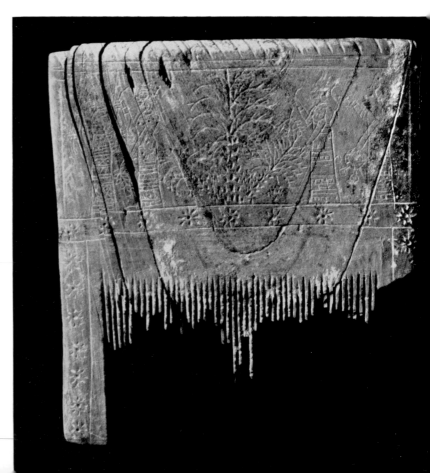

This small ivory box, forming part of a toilet-set, is decorated with
elaborate reliefs; female musicians entertain at a feast. Small boxes
like this were made of various materials. Usually there are several
compartments in them for the different kinds of make-up and the like.
Small bowls, too, for mixing make-up of diverse colours, as well as
other toilet utensils have been preserved.

45

Mask of a woman from the Mosul district. Oriental women not only emphasized the expression of their eyes by using a make-up of soot, pounded antimony, etc., but also liked to braid their black hair with coloured ribbons, threads and beads.

Beads of semi-precious stones and gold in various sizes are threaded here to form a necklace.

The lid of this ivory box found in Minet-el-Beida, the harbour district of Ugarit (14th/13th century B.C.), is decorated with the relief of a fertility goddess. Her charming pleated skirt reaching down to the ankles leaves the upper part of the body uncovered, as was the fashion in Crete at that time; the pattern of her pretty coiffure seems to hint at the same place of origin.

"*I am Napir-asu, the wife of Untash-napirisha. Whoever breaks my statue, or damages the inscription, is to be cursed by the great god . . .*" *This is the text of the inscription on the bronze statue of a queen of Elam (13th century B.C.). (45) She is represented in an embroidered, thinly woven garment.*

Spinning was a favourite occupation of noble women, too. Both the mistress and her servant have their hair carefully made up and wear embroidered garments. The costly furniture shows the high rank of the spinning woman. The stool on which she sits in a typically Eastern attitude is covered with soft material with fringes.

49

The mother goddess Ninchursag. An image of this popular goddess forms part even of the façade of an Elamic temple of the 12th century B.C., where she is represented in a relief.

The Kassite King Melishipak donated some land to his daughter Chunnubat-Nanā (12th century B.C.). This he did by introducing her to the goddess Nanā and by recommending her to the deity's special graces, as she was named by her name. The princess carries a lyre in her arm, indicating that she had been taught music, as was the custom in noble families.

The goddess Kubaba was worshipped as patron-goddess in Carchemish, an important Syro-Hittite town of the early 1st millennium B.C. She no doubt represents an aspect of the prehistoric mother-goddess. In the Greco-Roman period she was worshipped far and near by the name of Cybele. The worship of her was very popular.

"Neither the wives of citizens, nor widows, nor any Assyrian woman will uncover their heads when they go out into the street . . ." This is the wording of paragraph 40 dealing with the "veiling" of Assyrian women. On the clay tablet reproduced here are inscribed parts of the so-called "Women's Mirror", an important law code of the 12th century B.C.; it deals mainly with women's concerns.

This goddess from Tell Halaf originally stood on a lion and carried—together with two other gods, also standing on animals—part of the façade of a temple-palace. The builder had his name carved into her garment together with the following curse:

"Whoever defaces my name
And writes in its place his own name:
Seven of his sons shall be burned before the weather-god,
And seven of his daughters shall be handed
over to the goddess Ishtar as prostitutes."

55

56

Stela from the grave of a noble woman. It was an Aramaic custom to decorate the graves of their dead with stelae on which they themselves or their families were depicted. The noble rank of the spinning woman is indicated also indirectly by the scribe (her son?), as the art of writing was still a privilege of the upper layers of society.

Young scribe standing on his mother's lap. In the 8th to the 7th century the noble ladies wore dresses held together with belts and over them a wrap prettily edged with fringes. The attire of the son, the pride of the family, is particularly elegant. His writing utensils point to his abilities, and the attached bird to falconry.

Very fashionable at that period (8th/7th century B.C.) were the pins with which the garments were held together and decorated.

Married couple in loving embrace. The memory of their love was to be retained after their death. The wife has fastened a fibula at her belt — very fashionable at that time. In her hand she holds a mirror as a modern woman might carry her gloves; she has shoved the corners of her coat under her belt.

Hierodules of Astarte (?), the goddess of love. From a "Syrian window"—the window-sill rests on small columns—they look out at the street. Carefully attired and painted, they seem to be waiting for their lovers.

This relief of a woman seated on a throne forms the ornament of an ivory box. The rhomboid patterns on her dress point to artistic embroideries or to appliqué work.

61

King Esarhaddon and his mother Naqi'a, to whom he owed his throne. This unique relief of him together with his mother is proof of the high esteem in which he held the queen mother. Being a noble woman, she carries a mirror in her hand.

This small ivory work, showing a goddess, testifies to the high standard of the civilization at the courts of the 8th century B.C. Golden jewellery, precious stones, delicate woven fabrics, and sumptuous furniture formed part of the refined life of the upper circles.

Scenes of worship. Priestesses bring offerings to the goddesses. Certainly only people of high standing could afford to wear jewellery of

that kind, unless we assume that it was only used in the cult, for example, to decorate the deities' images.

At the approach of the victorious Assyrian King Sennacherib, a man with his two wives hides in the reeds, as did also many others of the natives. Another part of the relief shows the transportation of those who could not escape being made prisoners and who were distributed as workers to temples, palaces, and also to private households.

Transportation of women prisoners. The Assyrian kings often "described" in reliefs their victorious campaigns, frequently choosing the transportation of prisoners or other booty as a popular theme. The artists preferably recorded small and simple incidents, as, for example, here the loving care of a mother for her child.

Mirror. Its handle is formed by the figure of a nude woman. In ancient times delicately polished bronze mirrors were deemed very precious. Women of the upper classes liked to be depicted holding a mirror in their hand.

Tripod-candlestick in the shape of a woman.

King Ashurbanipal in the vine bower drinks to his wife Ashursharrat. The exalted couple is surrounded in the well-tended palace garden by numerous servants and entertained with music. Though the ceremonial of the court seems to be strictly observed, this relief is mainly the picture of a married couple harmoniously united. The celebration of the victory in resplendent autumn sun is bound to have offered a colourful and festive spectacle. Precious, richly embroidered blue and purple garments, golden jewellery, shining drinking bowls, carved furniture with gold and ivory ornaments, witness to the magnificence and the splendour of this royal court, where Queen Ashursharrat played rather an important role.

Prisoners are driven away. In the autumn, at the time of the grape harvest, their endless columns start on their long trek. On a two-wheeled cart two children hold on to their mother, who lovingly hugs the smaller one.

This head of a woman with the "archaic" smile on the lips has been called "Mona Lisa." It is an ornament on a piece of furniture. The man of the East has always been eager for adornment and liked to ornament all objects of daily use. Masterpieces of applied art were created especially at the courts.

The goddess Ishtar was not only the goddess of love to whom the hierodules of the temples dedicated themselves, but also the goddess of strife and war. As such she is here represented with quiver, bow and arrows, standing on a lion and worshipped by a praying woman.

Woman bathing in a tub. Bathing played an important role in the Ancient East, in religious observances as well as in everyday life. A "soap-plant" was used for cleaning; this, mixed with oil, was probably the most ancient soap. Quite often "baths" with an outlet for water have been discovered in houses, for instance, in Ashur and in Babylon.

Pregnant woman putting her hand in a protective gesture on her belly. This rather late Palestinian sculpture (6th to 4th century B.C.) is much younger than the pregnant goddess of Catalhuyuk of approximately 6200 B.C., shown above.

Wet nurse, seated with child at her breast. As children usually were breast-fed for a long time, the contracts with the wet nurses were made for two to three years.

These small plaques with representations of erotic scenes were found in an Ishtar temple at Ashur where the hierodules served the goddess of love. Benches built of bricks, like those shown in two illustrations, were used by the hierodules as supports and were excavated in several temples.

Women riding on mules. This scene is probably somehow connected with the cult of the dead; a cortège of women from the harem accompanies the deceased to his grave. Women used side-saddles and wore their usual dress. In ancient oriental art the first representations of riding women are from the 1st millennium B.C.

This Phrygian fertility goddess in a group of statues from Boghazköy is already greatly influenced by Greek art.

79

Parthian jewellery.

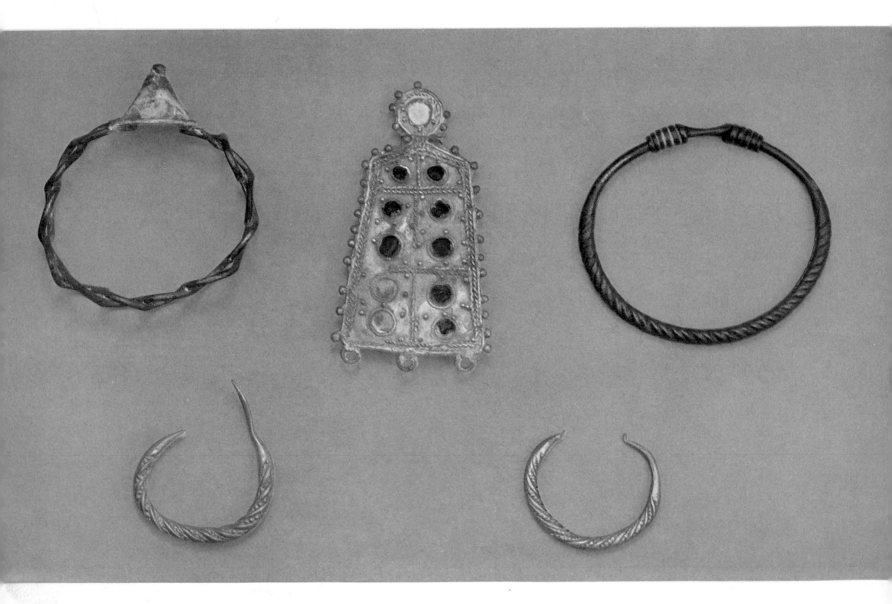

Statuette of standing goddess of love. She is shown nude but wearing jewellery and garnets set into her eyes and navel.

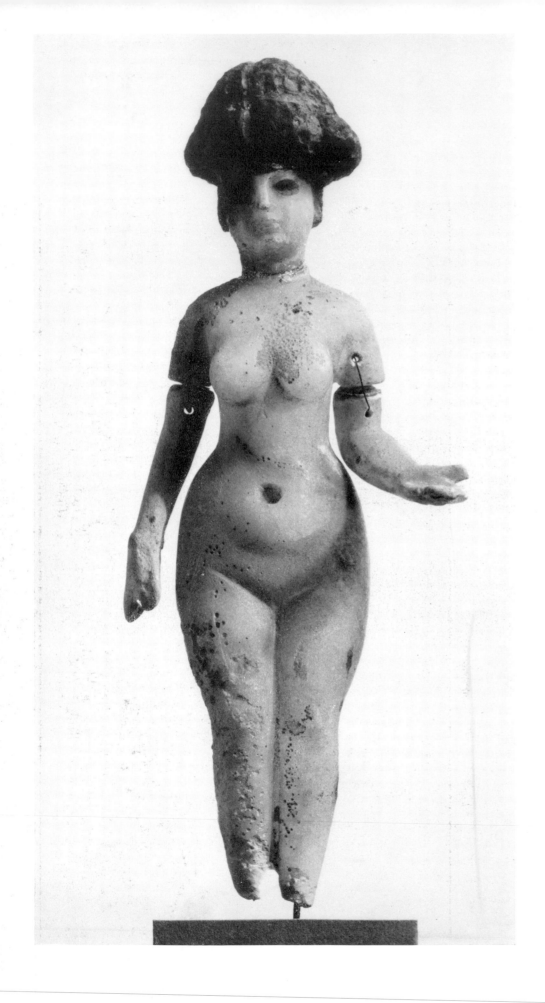

Sculptures of the nude Venus-Anahita. In connection with the cult of the goddess of love, the nude woman with her sensuous charms was shown again and again in various attitudes in applied art.

This nude woman, wearing jewellery and carrying a festive wreath in her hand, is doubtlessly connected with the cult of the fertility and love goddess.

Parthian-Sassanid coins: one of King Bahram I with his wife and the crown-prince (273–276 A.D.), one of Queen Buran (630–631 A.D.) and one of the Parthian Queen Thea Musa (2 B.C.–4 A.D.).

Portrait of a young girl. The artist, who with this expressive and noble head created an extremely beautiful work, was influenced by Greek as well as by Persian art.

Goddess of fert_____
breasts, a symb_____
again in this G_____

Parthian statuette of a woman, probably connected with the
Anahita cult.

Moses is rescued from the water by the Pharaoh's daughter. This
fresco from the synagogue of Dura Europos (250 A.D.) shows in
the centre the naked princess; three female servants are waiting for
her, carrying a box with jewellery and utensils for the care of the
body. To the left of the scene the rescued child is handed to its mother.

Funeral repast. This floor mosaic comes from a rock grave near Edessa. According to its Syrian inscription the grave was made at the order of a certain ZYDLT, son of Barbe'esmin, for himself and his children. The deceased, his wife, two daughters and four sons are shown in the mosaic. Costly family graves like this (see also the "grave towers" at Palmyra and Hatra) were often made for noble families.

95   *This alabaster relief still showing traces of an original coloured paint-ing represents the shapely bust of a young woman. The crescent of the moon shows that the goddess represented here is the moon goddess. Greek influence is evident.*

A noble Parthian standing before a goddess. There is nothing more to be seen here of the stiff frontal attitude typical of the old oriental gods. The posture of the goddess, with her hip bent outwards, definitely suggests Greek prototypes.

Tombstone bust of a woman from Palmyra, called Ammiat. Her costly jewellery and refined headgear indicate that she was wealthy.

This tombstone relief from Palmyra was erected in memory of a couple whose names are carved in the stone beside the heads in Palmyrene letters.

From a plate, showing in relief a funeral procession (?), the figures of three veiled women have been preserved. Walking in front of them, a camel carrying a sedan chair (tabernacle?). The plate was found in the temple of Baal at Palmyra.

Two female musicians on a camel. Seated in a kind of sedan chair, they play a double flute and a drum.

Head of a woman from Palmyra with the typical headdress of very thin material, fixed on to a fillet.

The goddess Ishtar. Greco-Roman influence characterizes this relief. Only the fact that she steps on an animal (or a man), thereby symbolizing her power, still points to the ancient oriental goddess of love and war.

Bust from the grave of an unknown woman in Palmyra. In the 1st century A.D. this town was a noteworthy trading centre, in particular much used for the distribution of goods brought there by caravans. The wealth of the inhabitants is mirrored in their works of art. In 271 A.D. under their beautiful and famous Queen Xenobia, they dared to fight the Roman empire, but were defeated by the Emperor Aurelian.

Lady from Palmyra. This relief perpetuating her memory, was made to close the grave which held her mummified body. She is represented in her usual luxurious and magnificent surroundings, with a servant carrying a jewellery casket.

Ubal, daughter of Jabal. The inscription on the stone on which she stands, records that the young woman died aged eighteen years, and that her husband had ordered this statue to be made in her memory.

"Denak, Great-Queen, first Lady of the harem," runs the inscription of this precious seal of which an impression is shown here. The Great-Queen, crowned and magnificently adorned, was the daughter of King Ardashir I, the founder of the Sassanid empire.

Female harpist. This floor mosaic was found in the magnificent palace, built by the Sassanid King Shapur in Bishapur. The mosaics of this room, probably used as a banqueting hall, represent ladies in waiting, bringing and wreathing flowers, dancing and making music.

Silver rhyton (drinking vessel) with head of a woman, probably of the goddess Dravspa, who was worshipped in the Irano-Indian area. The woman's head seems to be influenced by Indian art; the bull's head, also forming part of this rhyton, by Iranian art.

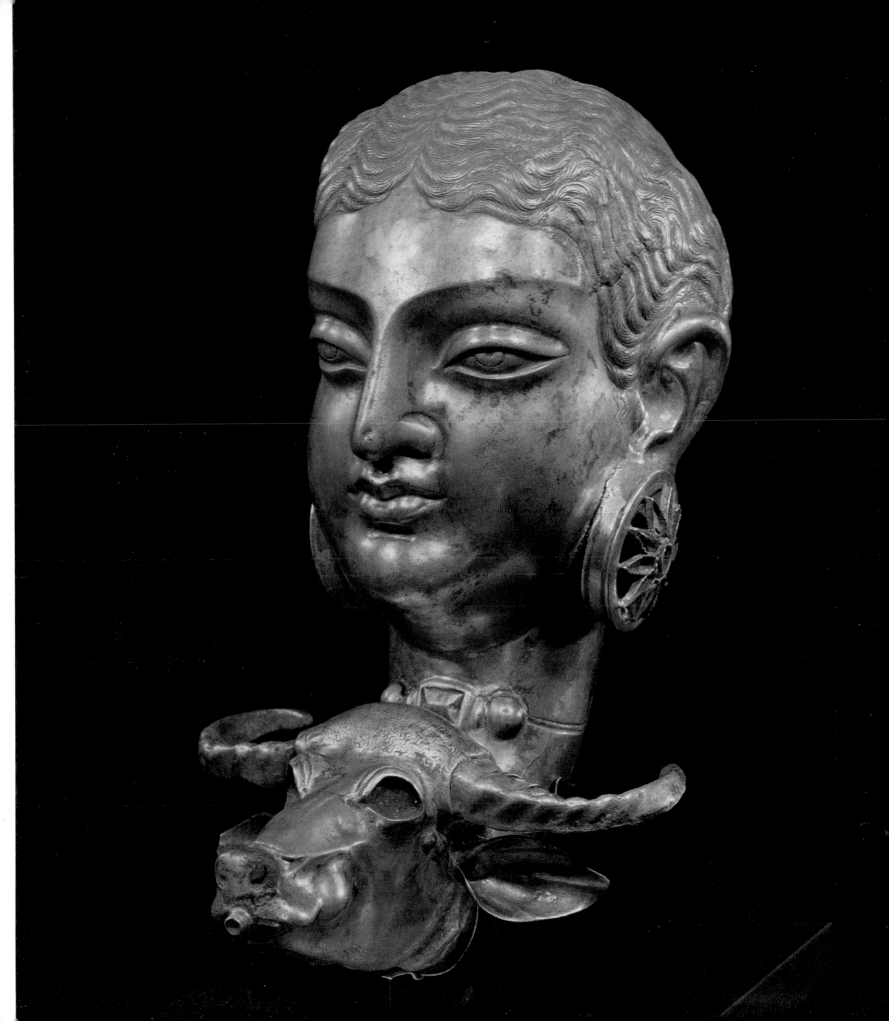

This arcade ornament in the shape of a young, beautiful moon goddess came from the Parthian temple in Hatra.

Sassanid silver vase showing the face of a woman.

The dancing goddess Anahita, represented as a fine and strong nude maiden, the female ideal of beauty of that period.

Four female dancers in transparent veil-like garments are shown dancing around on this precious gold and silver vase. The utensils which they hold in their hands were certainly intended for the cult of Anahita, whose servants the dancers probably were.

The royal banquet scene, represented on this bowl, shows that the queen took part in her husband's banquets. The boars' heads seem to indicate that this feast celebrates a successful hunt. The king sitting with his wife on a couch adorned with plump cushions, hands to her a festive wreath, part of the usual court ceremonies. More wreaths are lying in readiness to be given to guests.